T0061011

LEADERSHIP THROUGH GROUP PROCESS AND FACILITATING SKILLS

A TRAINING MANUAL FOR GROUP LEADERS

JOAN HALEY

Archway Publishing books may be ordered through booksellers or by contacting:

Archway Publishing
1663 Liberty Drive
Bloomington, IN 47403
www.archwaypublishing.com
1 (888) 242-5904

ISBN: 978-1-4808-8804-3 (sc)
ISBN: 978-1-4808-8805-0 (e)

Library of Congress Control Number: 2020902592

Print information available on the last page.

Archway Publishing rev. date: 05/29/2020

For Theeron

Leadership through Group Process and Facilitating Skills

If you identify with this cartoon as a group leader or
participant, this book is for you.

CONTENTS

Introduction 1

SECTION I: STRUCTURING THE GROUP

Chapter 1   Theory of the Group Process Formula® 9
Chapter 2   Stages of the Group Process Formula® 13
Chapter 3   Experiential Learning 31
Chapter 4   Imparting Knowledge 34
Chapter 5   Planning Your Group 40
Chapter 6   Working with a Co-leader 47

SECTION II: FACILITATING SKILLS

Chapter 7   Facilitating Skills to Maximize Learning 55
Chapter 8   Listening So People Talk 58
Chapter 9   Talking So People Listen 72
Chapter 10 Roadblocks to Effective Communication 81
Chapter 11 Nonverbal Behavior 85
Chapter 12 Additional Techniques for Effective Group
               Facilitation 89
Chapter 13 Tying It All Together 92
Chapter 14 Hooks and Games 94
Chapter 15 The Big Picture 101

JOAN E. HALEY, M.ED.

With a master's degree in adult education and training, Joan Haley has three decades of experience training community, corporate, and emerging leaders in group process and facilitating skills and has held executive and managerial positions for over two decades. In addition to serving on several nonprofit boards, Ms. Haley has been the executive director of nonprofit corporations including the Pittsburgh Schweitzer Fellows Program and the Parenting & Life Skills Institute. She is an experienced curriculum writer, group leader, teacher, and public speaker.

Ms. Haley developed the Group Process Formula®, which has been utilized by countless professionals and laypeople and has served as the model for many train-the-trainer programs. Joan Haley has a particular interest in essential skills for effective leadership and provides workshops across the nation regarding leadership.

Joan Haley is an avid reader of contemporary fiction, lover of blue grass and classical music, an experienced potter, and an advocate for children everywhere.

Joan Haley is a transplanted Pittsburgher and loves her city hard.

Visit our website for more information:
www.haleytraininginstitute.com

For more information about workshops, group process, or leadership, contact Joan Haley at, joan@haleytraininginstitute.com or (412) 508-6248.

INTRODUCTION

EFFECTIVE COMMUNICATION
AND GROUP PROCESS

While most of us don't think about it, whether we consider ourselves leaders or not, we are all group leaders in some way or another—whether you run board meetings, community groups, a family, or staff meetings or you teach. Therefore, the basics of how to structure groups and navigate group dynamics apply to much of our personal and professional lives.

Like you, I imagine, I have suffered through groups that were painfully boring, unenlightening, or out of control. On the other hand, and again like you I imagine, I have had the pleasure of being in groups that were wonderful. Some of those groups in each category were ones I have led. I knew it couldn't be just luck that some groups were magic and others a disaster. I figured the facilitator had to be a key to making or not making a group effective and enjoyable.

I have taught, led groups, and given presentations for most of my professional life. I studied adult education theory and training in my graduate program at the University of Pittsburgh. Still, I wasn't sure how to make all groups rewarding and change-making. I was, however, determined to find out, so I launched a pioneering effort to figure out two things about groups:

1. How to **structure a group** to maximize the learning of each participant, utilize the power of the group as a whole to bolster that learning, and make sure the participants left with newfound skills, attitudes, and behaviors to use in their lives.

2. How a leader effectively **facilitates learning** so that participants feel the group is a safe place to work through their own process of self-discovery and to make sure *all* participants are engaged in the group where mistakes are okay and nobody is going to monopolize the time, judge them, or put them down.

Although that seemed like a tall order, as an educator working with groups, providing presentations, and facilitating planning meetings, I had to tackle those two goals. *Leadership through Group Process and Facilitating Skills* is the result of that determined search to develop a new and distinct approach to lead effective groups and deliver dynamic presentations.

This book is divided into two parts, the first about structuring a group to maximize learning and the second, about employing effective facilitating skills to ensure all participants are engaged.

Group Process—Structuring the Group

Combining my experience with groups, adult education, and experiential learning, I have developed a structure for presenting material that is exciting and growth producing for leaders and participants alike. The conceptual framework is called the Group Process Formula® (GPF). The Group Process Formula is for people who work with groups of any kind, give presentations, or are involved in planning.

For me, developing the GPF as a conceptual framework for structuring a group was the result of decades of teaching, leading groups, and publicly speaking. In the process, I endured many battle scars that taught me what not to do, and I also scrutinized what worked to develop a failsafe structure for any group no matter the subject, the size of the group, or the reason for meeting. The emphasis is on how to teach, not what to teach. The result is a new and distinct approach for groups of any purpose, makeup, and size.

The Group Process Formula evolved from a shaky "If it works, use it, and we'll think about why later" into a mature ideational construct and conceptual framework for sequentially understanding the growth of the group as a whole and recognizing that true integration of newfound skills, knowledge, and attitudes is most often the result of recognizing learning as a human process that involves participants' feelings, experiences, and values rather than regarding it as a mechanical process involving only the transfer of knowledge.

The Formula reflects, too, my search for a way facilitators of learning can genuinely enjoy their groups, learn while they are leading, and truly do only fifty percent of the work. Facilitating means providing time and space for learning to happen for individual participants. As leaders, our responsibility stops with the dialectic of teaching; learning is an individual occurrence. Making the information one's own is a solo task for participants. This process of integration maximizes the potential for the learner to use his or her newfound knowledge.

The Group Process Formula delineates five stages for each session a group meets:

- Opener
- Foreshadowing
- Inductive
- Deductive
- Transition

The stages, which will be presented in detail later in this book, aim to encourage the maturation of any ongoing group no matter its purpose for meeting. The stages occur more or less sequentially during *each* session a group meets. As an outgrowth of my experience with groups and with teaching and learning, to date this framework is the most effective way to meet goals that I have for myself as a facilitator of learning, for the goals I have for participants in my groups to incorporate learning, and for conveying the subject matter I present.

The structure of the Group Process Formula aims to make the material come alive for participants and leaders. It increases awareness and positive changes in participants, which in turn encourages practical applications in their lives. In each session, there is an attempt to maintain a continuous unfolding for participants that hopefully will go on after the group ends. It is this rhythm that we, as facilitators, want to foster—coming to conclusions and forming questions, opening up to new information and then closing to integrate it, pushing complacency with the familiar, and inviting change to happen.

Facilitating participants' integration of material is the primary task of group leaders. The Formula corrals learning of a different quality and helps transform a group of people into a community of learners. For groups structured this way, there is a lot of interaction, energy, and reflection. Learning takes place within each participant in the group, as well as between participants. Energy and excitement are intrinsic to the process.

I have incorporated a variety of learning styles, teaching methods, and group process theories into the Group Process Formula, always combined with a strong belief that the lived experience is the best teacher for us all, with faith that the right answers for people lie within the individuals themselves, and with the knowledge that changing learners' behavior involves the confluence of human behaviors, values, feelings, and experiences with new information.

Through the use of the GPF, individual feelings and unique human experiences are highlighted, as are similarities and differences among participants' comments. It brings together the cognitive, affective, and experiential domains. The subject matter for the group becomes a meshing of the perceptions, experiences, and feelings of the people in the group with the material or information presented. The learning that takes place strikes a central chord in participants and is as unique as each individual in the room.

Knowing the subject matter is a must, but a quality leader needs more. Our emphasis is on how to teach, how to facilitate, and how to lead. We build skills, put theory into action and fortify people with newfound abilities to creatively plan, effectively lead meetings, and run groups. Participants gain concrete, practical strategies through active participation and feedback. By channeling healthy personal development and increased performance, participants incorporate relevant skills to use immediately in real-world situations.

Also in this first section, I have included a chapter on co-leading groups, which I highly recommend, though I know it can be a luxury in many settings. Utilizing this approach takes energy when the group meets and considerable planning before the group sessions occur. Having someone to share in the process can be fun and edifying for both leaders and participants. Additionally, I've included information about experiential learning and how people learn, and a section contrasting traditional teaching with effectively leading groups.

Facilitating Skills

The Facilitating Skills section, Section II, is again the result of decades of making mistakes and also hitting on the most effective way to communicate with group members to maximize their learning and that of the group as a whole. (Section I, remember, describes the Group Process Formula, a failsafe way of structuring a group to maximize participants' learning, engagement, and integration of skills to use in real-world settings.)

Structuring a group for maximal learning is essential, but it's not enough. We're encouraging participants to be engaged in the group as a whole, which means members of the group need to feel safe enough to engage in self-discovery, reflect on their own learning and insights, and figure out how to utilize the skills in their lives. I imagine, once again, that you have been in group settings where someone monopolizes the time, is overly critical, or loves to hear himself talk, or where only a few people in the group say anything.

In the Facilitating Skills section of this book, we present practical skills for the leader to use to make sure everyone is engaged, to draw people out, and to make sure potential monopolizers step back and typically quiet participants step up. We focus on increasing our understanding of why people do what they do in a group setting. We examine listening skills, techniques for confronting firmly and respectfully, and approaches to dealing effectively with people who "play games" in the group.

In Summary

Knowing the subject is a plus, but a quality leader needs more. The practical knowledge and how-to skills contained in *Leadership through Group Process and Facilitating Skills* will increase your leadership effectiveness—and it goes beyond steps and procedures. Our approach has evolved over many years, is tried-and-true, and is only available in *Leadership through Group Process and Facilitating Skills*. Utilizing the Group Process Formula and the facilitating skills presented herein will fortify your competence and confidence with newfound abilities to effectively facilitate groups and meetings and creatively plan.

Enjoy.

SECTION I: STRUCTURING THE GROUP

CHAPTER 1

THEORY OF THE GROUP PROCESS FORMULA®

In this chapter, we will examine the theory of the Group Process Formula as a structure for maximizing participants' integration of practical skills to change their behavior for the better. The personality of the group as it is formed over time is an important part of this dynamic learning process. Group facilitators using this approach believe that participants can make the best decisions for their lives. Our job is to facilitate their knowing that about themselves.

Forming the Group Personality
The Group Process Formula is an ideational construct and a conceptual framework for sequentially understanding the growth of a group's personality and for recognizing learning as a growth (and, therefore, change) process. Facilitating means providing time and space for learning to happen within the individual participant. Ideally, facilitators enjoy their groups and, like their participants, feel energized by the group.

Implementing the five stages of the Group Process Formula facilitates learning, and most learning involves a relationship. Much of the learning is going to happen through the leader's own genuineness, faith in group members, and comfort with the material.

The group's personality is unique for everyone and needs to be affirmed, rekindled, and recharged *every* session that the group meets. The members of the group need to feel and experience being a part of the group because the individual members (facilitators and participants alike) create the personality that is the group.

The attitude of a facilitator of learning is one of prizing the learners, valuing their opinions, and genuinely believing that all the participants in the group and their ideas are worthy of respect. This means stepping into their shoes and walking around, accepting their perspectives (which does not necessarily mean agreeing with that vision), and knowing them to be people who can make the best decisions for their lives. Our job is to facilitate their realizing this about themselves. This applies to facilitators of people of all ages and is essential for group leaders working with adult learners.

The feelings, experiences, and perspectives of the people in the group are as important as anything we teach. Highlighting participants' perspectives and experiences assists in the individual group members' integration of new material. The leader's posture is one of having information to communicate but not having the answers to how the participants will apply that information. Those answers lie within the individuals who make up the group.

Life Span of a Group

A group has a life span—a beginning, a middle, and an end. Groups change and grow like all living things. A group's life span is simply the length of time that a group will meet. During this life span, a group personality is formed. Whereas some groups die before their time, collapse, or become sick and nonfunctional, some groups thrive, gel, and grow. As group leaders, it is up to us to facilitate the formation of that personality, to foster the growth of the individuals who make up that personality, and to nourish the growth of the group as an entity.

Every human being is unique in his or her own way and is also similar to every other human being, and such is the case with groups. Groups develop in the way that individuals do. They, too, have crawling, walking, running, and sometimes flying stages. And like people, some groups come into the world frightened or deadpan and flourish in their adolescence. Some individuals come into the world fighting and kicking, and so can some groups.

With groups meeting over time with fairly consistent members, after three or four sessions we leaders probably have a pretty good picture of the personality before us. Growth occurs in the group as people become more aware and more effective at using their autonomy and interdependence. If all goes well, participants at this stage talk directly to each other rather than through the leader. That's a sign that participants are experiencing the group as their own.

My hope is that a group will end in late adolescence. By the time the group is in its adolescence, if all goes well, I usually have as much control of the group as one would over a big, brawny adolescent. The participants challenge, question, change the direction of the group and relish their independence. In the beginning, I figuratively hold participants' hands and direct and guide; by the last session, I consult and support.

Creating a climate in which participants change for the better and integrate skills and behaviors that will improve their lives is our goal. Utilizing what they have learned long after the group has ended—with participants (and leaders) healthily breaking away from the group, in which autonomy is felt and appreciated—is a goal for me.

I use the Group Process Formula to maximize that happening.

Key Points

- The Group Process Formula is a conceptual framework for sequentially understanding the growth of a group's personality and for recognizing learning as a process of change.
- Group leaders believe that participants can make the best decisions for their lives. Our job is to facilitate their knowing that about themselves.
- Group leaders facilitate the formation of the group's personality and foster the growth of the individuals who make up that personality.

CHAPTER 2

STAGES OF THE GROUP PROCESS FORMULA®

In chapter 2, we explain the five stages that make up the Group Process Formula—Opener, Foreshadowing, Inductive, Deductive, and Transition—as they relate to effective structuring of a group. By understanding these stages, the reader will be able to implement them to maximize the learning for participants in any group, no matter the reason for meeting.

Following the stages of the Group Process Formula every time the group meets is important to nourish the growth of the group, to maximize learning for each participant, and to recognize that the participants' experiences, perspectives, and feelings are just as important as the subject matter for each session. The stages are sequential and build on each other.

I am frequently asked why leaders need to utilize the five stages *every* time the group meets. Since so much learning takes place between participants, the identity of the group needs to be reinforced and nourished to maximize engagement and trust. Think of it this way: How would you feel if your partner decided that kissing you once a year was adequate to demonstrate his love for you? No. Relationships need to be consistently nourished, and so do groups.

Stage 1—Opener

To Start Your Group Sessions
The term *Opener,* as it is used in the Group Process Formula, refers to that brief part at the beginning of a session that helps people get to know one another better than they would if they were simply *x* number of people in the same room at the same time. The Opener starts the process of forming the personality of the group. It is similar to what is commonly known as an "icebreaker." The difference is that in addition to breaking the ice, the Opener meshes some information about participants as individuals (their feelings, experiences, and values about a certain topic) *with* the subject matter for the session.

The Opener is directed by the leader, who also participates in the exercise. It involves members of the group talking or doing something—perhaps in pairs or small groups or sometimes as a whole group. It is an experience that says, "We are participants in this group focusing on this subject matter."

Building Trust
In the first sessions, the main purpose of the Opener is that participants and leaders get acquainted quickly on a level more meaningful than they might otherwise experience and to learn everyone's names. The Opener is a way to efficiently and effectively establish trust in the group and to give permission for people to say anything they would like in the group setting, even if it is to one other person. It is essential that everyone in the group participates in the Opener—participants and leaders. Therefore, the Opener often takes the form of members talking to each other in pairs, trios, or small groups.

The Opener, as it is used in the GPF, is based on the belief that if an individual speaks to one or two other people in the group and is listened to and accepted, he is more likely to talk in the larger group. The Opener typically gets the adrenaline going, starts people thinking about the subject matter, and invites people to invest in the group process.

The facilitator does not teach in the Opener but simply sets up the exercise, which lasts no more than twenty minutes. In the Opener, we "touch it but don't teach it." What we want to teach comes later in the Deductive section of the GPF. The purpose of the Opener is to start participants thinking about the subject matter for the session. Openers also contribute to participants' establishing trust in the group as they get to know each other on a more meaningful level.

Addressing Excess Baggage
Sometimes the Opener can function as a way for participants to get rid of "excess baggage" so that they are clear to focus on the subject matter of the group. Excess baggage can take the form of confusion about last week's session, or something that's weighing on group members from home or work, or concern about the amount of snow that's falling outside—anything that might stand in the way of learning.

On October 27, 2018, in my hometown of Pittsburgh, eleven citizens were gunned down in their synagogue while they were worshipping. In addition to the eleven fatalities, six people were seriously wounded. All of Pittsburgh was reeling from this senseless tragedy, and leaders of groups that week developed Openers like, "Share with a partner your thoughts about the tragedy at the Tree of Life Synagogue." This Opener gave participants a chance to talk about something that was on everyone's mind before presenting the material for the session.

In later sessions, the Opener might be a homework review giving participants a chance to express concerns, successes, and nonsuccesses related to implementing the skills learned in the session.

The Importance of Openers
Within the first twenty to thirty minutes of each group session, the participants need to speak to at least one other person in the group. To make sure that happens we utilize Openers.

Openers help participants open up to their role as a member of the group and open their minds to information that will be presented to them later in the session.

But why is it important for people to *talk,* even to one other person, early in a session?

In their groundbreaking book, *Values and Teaching,* Louis Raths, Howard Kirschenbaum and Sidney Simon introduce a theory for clarifying values. One of the concepts they describe has always stuck with me – the power of what they call "publicly affirming" which simply means saying out loud your thoughts, feelings or perspective to someone else and having them accepted.

We all know the power of talking to friends, family, or even a stranger when we're wrestling with a decision or confused about a situation. This belief in the power of simply talking is at the heart of many therapies.

Howie Kirschenbaum puts it this way in *Advanced Values Clarification:*

"To the extend that we can make our needs, thoughts, values or desires known to others, we increase the probability of clarifying them for ourselves. Appropriate sharing of our feelings and thoughts increases that probability when we see how others respond to us and how we respond to our own public affirmation of our inner world. We, therefore, learn more about ourselves, our goals and what is meaningful for us."[1]

---

[1] *Advanced Values Clarification,* Howard Kirschenbaum, 1977, p.11

Examples of Structures for Openers

I have seen group leaders very effectively develop fairly simple Openers by having members of the group share their experience with another person about implementing the skills that were presented in the last session, or talk with a partner about any thoughts that occurred to them regarding the information from the last session. Remember the purpose of the Opener is to have people share and start thinking about the topic of the group. The paired activities just described do meet those two goals.

There are many other ways to structure Openers that can be edifying and fun. With that in mind, I will provide examples to give you an idea of how the structure of some Openers might look; the *content* is dictated by you. There are many other possibilities for structuring an Opener—use your imagination.

- **Rank Ordering**

Rank ordering can create a lot of interest and questions in the group. It highlights similarities and differences among group participants. Often people are surprised that their fellow group members rank order differently than they do. Even though rank ordering stimulates questions and comments, remember that if this activity is used as an Opener, you don't encourage lengthy discussions and comments.

Here's an example of rank ordering:

What's most important to you in a job?

- o   salary
- o   camaraderie of colleagues
- o   autonomy
- o   title
- o   flexibility

Ask the group to individually write down the rank order of these examples according to what's most important to them to least important, with number one being the most important for them. After participants have written down their rank ordering silently, get responses from the participants via a show of hands, saying, "How many of you ranked *salary* as number one, as number two, as number three?" and then do the same for each item. Writing these on a board or flip chart so participants can see the difference in ranking among members of the group is important and illustrates the differences in opinions we all have.

Because an underpinning of all group sessions is to highlight similarities and differences, I would point that out in this exercise – particularly the people who rank ordered the five items very differently.

Sometimes I ask participants, after highlighting the differences in the way people have rank ordered, *"Which one of us has the right answer?"* This brings to mind for participants that there are many ways of viewing the same event, circumstance, experience, or exercise and hopefully opens their minds to different points of view. We need to be reminded of this. Too often we think everyone thinks the way we do.

- **Values Voting**

Values voting can be utilized over and over again—just change the content of the questions. Ask all participants questions that are not factually based but, rather, that elicit the opinions or values participants hold. Participants "vote" silently on the answers to the questions by raising their hands if they agree and putting their thumbs down if they do not agree. If they strongly agree, they raise their hands and swirl them, and if they strongly disagree, they put their thumbs down and swirl them.

Ask ten to fifteen questions for this exercise and tell participants not to talk while doing this, but rather to look around to see how others vote.

All questions need to begin with "How many of you …?"

For example:

"How many of you think most women get paid the same as men holding the same position?"

"How many of you would enjoy jumping from an airplane with a parachute?"

"How many of you felt good this week about implementing the skills we discussed in our group last week?"

- **Forced Choice**

Forced choice gets participants up and moving, which is always a good idea in a group. Again, it's interesting for participants to see how differently their fellow group members feel about given topics.

Here's how you set up the exercise.

Have participants stand in the middle of the room clumped together, and indicate "extremes" by pointing to either side of the room and asking participants to go to one side or the other according to how they identify with one of the two extremes. Participants need to walk to either side without talking and cannot stand in the middle.

For example, say to participants, "Are you more of a picky eater (pointing to one side of the room), or will you eat anything (pointing to the opposite side of the room)"? Then ask participants to walk to the side of the room they identify with more.

Take two or three explanations from participants from either side about why they chose to stand on that particular side, and leave it at that. Remember: touch it, don't teach it. No one can stand in the middle.

Ask people to congregate in the middle of the room again. People can get "lazy" and just stay on one side if you do not ask them to move back to the middle.

Here's another example (this one uses metaphors): "Are you more of a rhinoceros or an ostrich?" Point to either side of the room, indicating where participants need to stand according to which metaphor they identify with more.

Often participants will say, "What? What do you mean?"

As a group leader, your answer is, "Whatever occurs to you."

- **Continuum**

Continuum is a variation on forced choice where you paint two extremes. The difference is participants stand on a continuum or line to indicate gradations of how they feel about a given issue rather than choosing one or another extreme. Participants stand together in the middle once again.

For example, you as the leader might say, "Where do you stand on the issue of the clothes you wear? At one end, you are the type of person who cuts holes in her clothes when they are new, and at the other end of the continuum you love clothes, have a lot of them, look neat, and always dress appropriately. Where do you stand on this continuum when it comes to the clothes you wear?"

Other examples are continua about being or not being a "political junky" or how people feel about socializing or being alone. Or you could use even more controversial topics such as how you feel about socialized medicine or abortion. Do not use highly charged topics like these unless you know trust has been built in the group and participants' opinions will be respected.

Again, make sure you ask people to come back to the middle before setting up another continuum—and again, no one can stand in the middle. We don't want any compulsive moderates.

- **Unfinished Sentences**

Unfinished sentences can be used as an Opener to get a quick picture of where participants are or as a transition activity as a way for participants to reflect on what they have learned during the session. Generally, unfinished sentences are used with the entire group, but they could be used in small groups as well.

Have participants—all of them or just a few—finish a sentence stem. I generally ask anyone who wants to finish the stem to jump in. Everyone in the group will probably identify with responses from a few of the participants.

Here are some examples:

- "Something I want to take from today's session is ..."
- "Sometimes I wish ..."
- "Something I'd like to do this year is ..."
- "A highlight of my week leading a staff meeting was ..."

- **High Point / Low Point**

For the exercise, high point / low point, have participants share in pairs or trios the high point of their week and a low point of their week.

Be sure to have each participant in the pair or trio share in turn first his high point and then for the second round, the low point.

Ask for 2-3 people to share with the whole group what they described for either the high point or low point. Ask the group then, "Which came to mind more easily – your high point or low point?"

Usually participants say their low point. Point out how "low points" are more frequently noticed in our society – we're paid by insurance companies when we are sick, not when we are well; teachers often put the number wrong at the top of an assignment rather than the number right; rarely do we hear on the news positive and uplifting stories, but rather disasters and negative ones.

- **Take a Stand**

Take a stand is another activity that gets people moving.

The facilitator posts quotes or metaphors around the room and asks participants to stand next to the quote with which they most identify. All quotes in some way relate to the subject matter for the session.

Ask people to go *silently* to the quote and stand next to the one they most identify with. Say to them, "Think of a specific example that comes to mind for the quote you choose."

Here are examples of quotes we placed around the room for a workshop in leadership where people "took a stand" with the one they identified the most.

"Never doubt a small group of thoughtful committed citizens can change the world. Indeed it is the only thing that ever has." Margaret Meade

"A leader is a dealer of hope." Napoleon Bonaparte

"Well behaved women rarely make history." Anonymous

"My best successes came on the heels of failures." Barbara Corcoran

Ask members of the group who have chosen the same quote to talk to each other about what the quote means to them. After they have shared with each other, ask for 3-4 people to tell the whole group how the quote they chose resonated for them.[2]

Stage 2—Foreshadowing

Clear Directions
The Formula is more or less sequential, each session starting with an Opener and ending with the Transition. Foreshadowing can occur several times during a session. It is a statement of transition or a "grounding" for participants about why the group is doing what it is doing. Foreshadowing can be a statement of goals or expectations. It provides parameters for people before they actually do an exercise or group activity. The leader will state what is to be done, why group members are doing it, and how it will be used.

For example you might say,

"For this exercise, please pair with someone in the room you don't know and talk about how you used the skills we discussed in last week's session during this past week. Each of you will have five minutes. I will call time after ten minutes so space yourself."

Continue with the following directions:

"After this activity, I'd like to hear from everyone about their experience with the skills we introduced last week that you tried out at home or work during the week." Or you might say, "Let's hear from three or four people about what it was like this week trying out the skills we introduced last week."

---

[2] I have presented these possible structures for Openers in my own words. The inspiration for some of these exercises came from *Values Clarification* by Sidney B. Simon, Leland W. Howe, and Howard Kirshenbaum (New York: Grand Central Publishing, 1995).

Foreshadowing provides safety in the group because directions are clear and thorough.

Comfort and Caring

Foreshadowing also answers "comfort" questions for participants such as, "Is this a lecture class?"; "Can we ask questions whenever we want, or should we save them until the end?"; "Can we only get coffee on the break, or may we do so anytime during the session?"; "Will we start and end on time?"; and "Where are the bathrooms?"

It is important for leaders to address these issues in the first session whether people ask or not. Also, provide an overview of the entire class. Let's say you are planning to meet for six sessions, provide an overview of topics for each session during the first meeting so participants have a sense of the entire class or workshop.

A Bridge

Foreshadowing, too, is used as a bridge looking back to where the group has been and forward to where it is going. The term is used to touch on what is to come next, not explaining it or teaching it but giving an idea about what is going to happen. Foreshadowing can sometimes be a "dangling of the carrot"—raising interest about what is to come next.

For example you might say,

"For our first two sessions we will discuss leadership traits and characteristics. For the remaining four sessions we will describe and demonstrate concrete skills most exemplary leaders utilize and will practice the skills in class."

Stage 3—Inductive

Developing the Stage

The leader plans, creates, and initiates the Inductive part for each session a group meets. The meat of the Inductive phase of a group comes from the participants. It is usually an exercise that is geared toward calling forth something that participants already know about the subject matter for the session. The specific information that leaders want to give will come later in the Deductive stage of the Group Process Formula.

Participant Experiences

The Inductive section of the group attempts to bring into awareness experiences of participants that dovetail with the subject matter for the session. It needs to be an exercise that will resonate to some degree with everyone in the room. Therefore, as leaders, we need to establish the Inductive exercise by thinking of a prompt that is a statement or question to which everyone can relate.

For the Inductive stage, you want to think of an exercise that will make the subject matter come alive for participants. For example, in a parenting class on "Setting Effective Rules for Children," you might ask participants to describe "musts" or "have-tos" in their families when they were children. Or if the topic for a session is "Annual Staff Evaluations," you might develop an Inductive like "Describe a time someone gave you valuable feedback about a job you completed." With these examples, you can guess that everyone has an experience that will come to mind, whether they share that experience or not with the group. It is only necessary for a few group members to verbalize their experiences in the Inductive phase of the group.

Participants' responses to the Inductive exercise most often are descriptive; they describe their experiences in response to the Inductive prompt, which is something we encourage. This gives the leader "fodder" to tie participants' descriptive experiences in with the teaching points the leader wants to make that directly relate to the subject matter for the session.

The Inductive stage of the Group Process Formula is a way of tapping into what individuals already know about the subject matter. It is the acknowledgment that everyone has information, experiences, and feelings on some level about virtually any topic and that when those experiences join with the information that will be presented later, there will be increased motivation for learning and for utilization of material. This is particularly true for the adult learner.

Common Denominator

The question for the leader in creating the Inductive is "What common denominator experience can I tap into that touches in some way on the subject matter and demonstrates that participants already have a wealth of ideas, experiences, and feelings about the topic for the day, whether the topic is 'Positive and Negative Effects of Power,' 'How to Write a Progress Report', or 'Speaking Effectively in Public'?"

Participants' Relationship to the Subject Matter

The Inductive part of each session is based on the belief that some facet of any subject can be highlighted to create an experience for participants to better know themselves as they relate to the subject. It reflects the belief that an important component (if not the most important component) of learning is that it be experiential, that it can be lived. We do not teach by grafting on to our participants or by pouring our pearls of wisdom into the empty vessels before us. Rather we facilitate a dovetailing of what we want to communicate and what the learner's experience and perspective are as we look together at material.

The Inductive exercise aims to point participants in a direction that is meaningful for them with each learner going after what she feels is meaningful to learn about the subject. The individual participant's already existing relationship to the subject matter is what the leader attempts to bring into awareness in the Inductive section of the Group Process Formula. The responses are individual for each member of the group and equally as varied.

Once a few people have shared their experiences, be sure to highlight what the members of the group have shared and how it ties into the subject you are presenting. This process motivates people to take in the information you will present in the Deductive section of the session.

Because participants realize they already know something about the subject matter, they most often are poised to hear what you will present.

I recently attended a docent tour of a new collection at the Carnegie Museum of Art in Pittsburgh, and the docent started the tour by asking us to share a time when a painting or picture bowled us over. I thought, *That's a perfect Inductive!* People shared examples like: "The painting made me smile."; "It reminded me of a joyful time from childhood."; and "The look on the boy's face in that painting made me think of injustices in the world." After we had shared our experiences and why we were bowled over, the docent said, "I think that's exactly what you will experience today with this new exhibit. It will touch you deeply." Wow, were we excited to see it! And that was a good tie-up to the Inductive, by the way.

The Inductive exercise can be difficult to develop. It's worth the time and effort and can be a turning point in the group in terms of participants' openness to the information you will present and the possibility of its usefulness to improve their lives.

Stage 4—Deductive

The Deductive stage usually has two parts—the Deductive information and the Deductive exercise. The Deductive information involves the leader presenting didactic information about the subject for the session. The Deductive stage, too, is the tying together of what participants expressed in the Inductive exercise and what the leader is presenting about the topic.

Practice
The Deductive exercise is the culminating activity where participants "try on" the new skill. It is an opportunity for participants to see how the new material fits and feels for them in the laboratory setting of the group before they try it out in their real-world settings. This exercise is a chance for people to test the waters as they relate to the new material.

The Deductive exercise begins the process of integration of the material that hopefully continues long after the group ends. Here we are asking participants to be actively involved with the new information, to use that information, and to change in some way.

Shifting Perspectives

Participants are often shifting from one perspective to another in this part of the session. As participants experiment with exercises using newfound skills and information, they often make statements such as, "This won't work with my students (or children, colleagues, or friends)," or "Wow, this is great!" This can be as frightening as it is exciting. The changes can happen subtly or with explosions.

After having "tried on" the new material, participants may resist using it or question its relevance to them. This resistance is a natural part of people's changing. As facilitators of learning, we are asking participants to extend themselves beyond the familiarity of what they know and to utilize the strangeness of new material. Implicitly we are asking them to entertain change because the expectation is the utilization of the material. We are asking people to assimilate this new perspective in such a way that is alive for them, and we expect that they will eventually make it their own.

Stage 5—Transition

The Transition stage of the Group Process Formula focuses the attention of participants outside the group and asks them to use what they have learned in the group in the real world. It is the process that they have experienced in the Deductive exercise extended into their everyday lives. Transition most often takes the form of trying out the skills or information they have learned in the session in their real-world situations. It is an invitation to experience oneself in a new way in the everyday world.

In each session, there is an attempt to make that continuous unfolding happen, and this hopefully goes on long after the group ends. It is the rhythm that we want to keep alive—the coming to conclusions and forming questions; the opening up to new information then closing to integrate it; the being in familiarity, pushing gently on that familiarity, and inviting newness to enter.

Key Points

- Knowing subject matter is important, but it's not enough.
- The stages in the Group Process Formula occur sequentially and need to be implemented every time the group meets.
- The Opener builds trust in the group and helps participants start to think about the subject matter.
- The Inductive involves the subject matter the leader is presenting along with participants' perspectives, experiences, and feelings.

CHAPTER 3

EXPERIENTIAL LEARNING

The Group Process Formula is based on experiential learning where participants' perceptions, experiences, and feelings are meshed with the content for the session. As an educator, leader, and public speaker, I have seen over and over again the power of experiential learning as the most dynamic approach for people to integrate skills and knowledge and change their behavior, their attitudes, and sometimes their values. This type of learning is at the heart of the Group Process Formula.

With the Group Process Formula, participants are active in every session and contribute their own experiences, perceptions, thoughts, values, and feelings to the content presented. Sometimes we also aim to stimulate the senses, use metaphors and storytelling, provide hypothetical situations or scenarios, access emotions and imagination, or request observation and silence.

With our overarching goal of changing the participants' attitude, behavior, and thinking, we know experiential approaches are the most powerful tools for change making—and they make learning so much fun.

There are a variety of approaches to learning that can be experiential. Here are a few that are considered experiential approaches to learning.

New Experience

When we speak of experiential learning, most people think of the immersion in a new experience like an internship, fellowship, or semester abroad. These opportunities provide a wealth of new learning for the participant. Reflection in the form of journals or debriefing is often a part of the experience. People participating in the Peace Corps report, even decades later, the experience as life changing.

Utilizing the Group Process Formula provides "new experiences" in the group setting by using role-playing, hypothetical situations, small groups, exercises, and activities. Participants in groups using the Group Process Formula talk and move around a lot during a session.

We involve the learner in experiences with the goal of observation, reflection, and possible change. We utilize elements such as action, reflection, and transfer.

Hands-On Learning

Using or constructing physical objects is another form of experiential learning. The learner is learning by doing, whether it is how to throw a pot on a potter's wheel, how to implement advanced Excel skills, or how to assemble a piece of IKEA furniture. Most often this type of learning does not involve reflecting on the experience.

We sometimes use physical objects to advance learning. For example, you might ask participants to rank order five items from worst to best on a sheet of paper, or use a prop that symbolizes a particular point you want to make about the subject matter. Any PowerPoint or video, just as long as it is pictorial (rather than just words), can be used to advance learning.

One of my favorite ways to use physical objects is using storyboards for Compression Planning® exercises. Compression Planning is an effective and efficient way to plan utilizing a broad base of constituents to brainstorm ideas that fall into several categories. The goal is to have a good enough plan *now* rather than a perfect plan in nine months. Compression Planning is an action-oriented process used in many settings for efficient problem solving or strategic planning. As the founder used to say, "It's for people who want to get stuff done."

I had the privilege of learning this approach from the founder, Jerry McNellis, three decades ago and have regularly used Compression Planning ever since.

Practice

Everyone knows that through practice we learn to do something well— to serve a tennis ball, to ride a bike, to execute a dance step.

In the Deductive stage of the Group Process Formula, we provide time for participants to "try on" what they've learned before they implement the skill in their lives. This is another example of experiential learning. The experience provides participants with feedback about how they have integrated a skill and gives them a chance to tweak approaches if necessary.

Practicing is a way for participants to become more self-aware and helps them transform the experience into something meaningful and useful to them. Practicing what has been presented in class or in the group is a type of experiential learning since participants are trying on what they have learned before they utilize the newfound skills and information in their personal or professional lives.

Expect that each member of the group will respond to the new information and skills presented in different ways and to varying degrees of acceptance. People have to chart their own journey of self-discovery.

CHAPTER 4

IMPARTING KNOWLEDGE

Sometimes people have asked me how what we do with the Group Process Formula is different from traditional classroom learning and whether this approach can be utilized for presentations and other types of public speaking. The GPF approach can most definitely be used for any presentation or speaking event.

In this chapter, you will find some charts that delineate similarities and differences between several types of learning where a leader, teacher, instructor, or consultant is involved.

All of us have learned in a variety of ways—through experience, maybe by memorizing facts, by being inspired by a profound speaker, by reading, or perhaps even by watching someone doing something, or reading step-by-step directions.

There are several ways people learn in group settings and probably many more for solitary learning. Below is an overview of ways people learn from a leader, teacher, or consultant—vehicles for imparting knowledge: consulting, presentations, teaching, and facilitating. I also have included a comparison between traditional classroom teaching and facilitating as a group leader.

Here are four major categories to impart knowledge:

- Consulting
- Presentations
- Classroom teaching/lecturing
- Facilitating/training

I. Consulting—providing information to better the performance of another person

Relationship: consultant–consultee

- o Consultant and consultee seen as equals
- o Have respect for each other's knowledge
- o No hierarchy
- o Possible impact to change behaviors or attitudes, but this is up to consultee
- o Consultee open to, but not dependent on, consultant
- o Consultee-initiated
- o Most often little feedback about performance
- o Usually individual or small group
- o Usually brief meetings

Motivation: advice

II. Presentations—usually a one-to-three hour talk with people interested in the topic

Relationship: presenter–audience

- o Most often "one shot"
- o Presenter-centered

- o Not usually interactive, though there might be questions and answers
- o Most often people are not required to attend
- o Size of group not important
- o Usually low impact to change behaviors and attitudes
- o Potential for high degree of raising awareness
- o Audience not dependent on presenter
- o Most often no feedback

Motivation: usually interest

III. Classroom teaching/lecturing—passing on knowledge to students, usually in a classroom

Relationship: teacher–student

- o Teacher plans and directs
- o Students most often receptive, perhaps passive learners
- o Grades, tests, papers most often used
- o Teacher—the expert
- o Student needs something from teacher such as grades or credit
- o Imparting information—primary focus, often the only focus
- o Evaluation, judgment
- o Benchmarks: tests, papers
- o Emphasis on knowing information, not necessarily using information
- o Can range from totally lecture with no one knowing anyone in class to interactive
- o Different teaching methods often used
- o Most often learning subject matter is the assumed outcome
- o Feedback important
- o Homework often given by teacher

Motivation: grades, credit, interest

IV. Facilitation/training—usually ongoing with the emphasis on practical application

Relationship: facilitator–participant

- o High impact to change behavior and attitudes
- o Facilitator plans and directs
- o Participant-centered
- o Highly interactive
- o Practical—people use information immediately
- o Bridges to the next session (homework)
- o Ongoing meetings—usually weekly
- o Part of the content is the people, their experiences, and their perspectives
- o Skills orientation
- o Facilitator seeks to foster the independence of the participant by focusing on ways for him or her to integrate material
- o Climate: upbeat, positive, fun
- o Many different modalities for learning and group configurations
- o Perception: group with an identity
- o Size: usually six to fifty or more
- o Often fast-paced
- o Ideally co-led
- o Participants rarely required to participate or called on
- o Facilitators and participants seen as contributing to the subject matter to be learned; the knowledge and experience participants have is utilized as part of the curriculum
- o Participants go at their own pace
- o Motivation/learning styles addressed
- o Engagement in the group is part of the learning
- o Skills integrated by individuals
- o No grades or judgment
- o Benchmarks: oral and written personal reflections and commitments
- o All participate, even facilitators

Motivation: to do something better

Facilitating a Group and Classroom Teaching

Another way to look at the difference between many traditional ways of learning and what we recommend with the Group Process Formula can be found in the following chart.

Effective Facilitating as a Group Leader	Teaching as a Classroom Teacher and Coach
Facilitator plans, directs, organizes curriculum and teaching modalities	**Teacher** plans, directs, organizes curriculum and teaching modalities
Goals and objectives are articulated for each session and may change as a result of what transpired during the previous session with participants	**Goals and objectives** are articulated, and may not change from class to class
Recipient of training most often perceives himself or herself as a part of a group	**Recipient of teaching** most often perceives himself or herself as a student
Participant-centered: facilitator paces curriculum according to the needs of participants	**Teacher-centered:** teacher does most of the teaching during sessions
Purpose: to change participants' behavior and/or attitudes as they relate to content	**Purpose:** to increase recipients' knowledge of content
Frequent change in teaching modalities	Most often, **infrequent changes** in teaching modalities
Goal: practical—for recipients to use information and skills in their lives	**Goal:** recipients gain knowledge and may or may not use information
Experiential homework—recipients "trying it out" in their real-world setting	**Homework**—usually writing or reading
Curriculum: the knowledge, experiences, and beliefs of participants are perceived and utilized as part of the curriculum	**Curriculum:** Information-and content-oriented
Skills-oriented—participants are learning to do something or learning to do something better	**Information-oriented**—recipients are learning about something
Climate: upbeat, positive, fun, sometimes noisy	**Climate:** usually recipients are passive and quiet
Interaction encouraged and seen as an important part of learning	**Interaction** between students often **discouraged**
Ideally **co-led**	Often a **single instructor**

No "**requirements**," though there is "built in" expectation and "peer pressure." No tests, papers, evaluations

Focus: content meshed with participants' experiences, values, and perceptions for skills integration

Benchmarks: Many checks and balances along the way to see if participants have understood and integrated material

Culminating evaluation by participants to gauge how information and skills can be used in their lives and possibly oral and written reflections and commitments

Requirements expected; possible pressure from teacher to learn

Focus: information acquisition

Benchmarks: Grades, credit, tests, evaluations, attendance to check students' learning

Culminating evaluation by students is usually a paper, quiz, or test

CHAPTER 5

PLANNING YOUR GROUP

Most of the work for the group facilitator needs to happen when she is planning the group session before the group meets. It is important for a leader to establish goals and have an overall picture of what she wants to accomplish before the session starts. This will free up the leader to genuinely facilitate the group when they meet.

In this chapter, we will go over the steps a group facilitator needs to take to effectively plan for the group.

As a group leader, do the following each session:

- Establish **goals** for the session. Two or three is plenty. Make them in terms of *your* goals for your participants, what objectives you hope will be met by the end of the session (to _____ (verb)).

  For example: - To practice the three steps in confronting employees sensitively and firmly.

- Prepare an **agenda** for the group for the entire course. The agenda often focuses participation on the overall plan and can provide comfort for the participants in terms of "Where do we go from here?"

- Follow the **five stages of the Group Process Formula**.

- Decide what **Opener** you will use and how much time it will take.

- Most of your energy will probably center on the **Inductive** part. Use your creativity, intuition, and imagination. Try out your Inductive exercise on your co-leader, colleague, or partner—anyone—to see if they will give the answers to your Inductive prompt that you expect and want.

- Establish what **information (Deductive** part) you want to present. What information about the topic do you feel is necessary and important to give your participants for each session? What do you want to present in your Deductive section? Did your Inductive help you get to the information you want to present in the Deductive part?

  Be realistic about how much information your group can absorb during the session. Remember: the goal is not to have them absorb as many facts as possible, but rather to understand new information in order to integrate it to change behavior.

- During the Deductive part of the session, use **personal examples**. Share examples about yourself when developing the material for your session. Tell your group how the subject matter is important to you and how it resonates for you. Let them experience your humanness. You cannot use too many personal examples of successes and nonsuccesses. Stories stick with people.

- Decide what the **Deductive exercise** will be and how you will ensure that all participants are involved in practicing the skill or approach related in the Deductive information you presented.

- Every step of the way, ask yourself, "Does this information, this exercise, and/or this personal example help me **get to my goals**?" If the answer is no, then don't use the information, exercise, and/ or personal example.

- Anticipate how your participants will react to your information and exercises. Think of your **worst-case scenario and best-case scenario** of how they will respond. Discuss this with your co-leader.

An Example of How to Plan a Session

Topic: Setting Rules for Children
Co-leaders: Susie Smith and Fred Jones
Group name: Parents of Toddlers Meeting at Magee Hospital
Date and time: Wednesday, February 2, 7:00–9:00 p.m.

Stage 1—Opener

The leader says to the group, "In pairs, for ten minutes share a rule you experience in your daily life that you are thankful for, and discuss why you are thankful for it. Choose the person in the group whom you know least of all. Each of you will have five minutes to share."

Stage 2—Foreshadowing

The co-leaders share the following goals for the session with participants:

- To have all participants practice rule setting utilizing the three criteria.
- To raise participants' awareness of the three elements for successful rule setting via concrete examples.

Stage 3—Inductive

Since the topic for this session is on rule setting, the co-leaders need to ask a question of participants that will mesh their experience about rules with some of the information the leaders will present in the Deductive about effective rule setting.

Here is the Inductive exercise the leaders developed for this session:

"Think of something you had to do as a child that really annoyed you. Tell us how you felt about it and what you did (that is whether you complied with it or did not.)"

Continue with the following directions to the group: "I'd like to hear from three or four of you about what comes to mind. I'll write your responses on the poster paper."

Tie up the Inductive and mesh it with the information you want to convey in the Deductive.

Stage 4—Deductive

This is the stage in the Group Process Formula where the leaders present new information to the participants. This new information is didactic information, and this stage is the closest leaders using the GPF will get to traditional teaching or lecturing.

Deductive Information
The leader says to the group, "Today we are going to talk about effective rule setting to change unwanted behavior in one of your children. Later on you will decide what behavior you want to change, and then we will talk about how you are going to do this before you leave this session."

Here is the didactic information the leader provides for the participants:

"Rule setting means setting limits on a child so that learning can occur. The goal in rule setting is to change a behavior. A behavior is something you can hear a person say or something that you see him or her do. For example, throwing toys and name-calling are behaviors. For our purposes in this course, for a rule to be successful, it must be definable, reasonable, and enforceable. A rule is stated in behavioral terms."

To be effective, a rule needs to be definable, reasonable, and enforceable.

Definable means parents must be specific in what they want the child to do. For example, if the rule is "clean your room," spell out when and exactly what cleaning a room means to you. Does it involve making the bed? Are clothes put away where they belong (or just shoved into the closet)? Are toys put away (or pushed under the bed)? Give details about what you mean.

Reasonable means that the rule must be within the child's physical and mental capabilities. Don't ask a three-year-old to empty a wastebasket that is bigger than he or she is. The rule should take other family members into consideration. For example, having a child practice the piano at a time when Dad watches the news on TV may merely exchange one problem for another.

Enforceable means that there is a time limit on the rule so that you know when it has or has not been accomplished. For example, "Your room must be cleaned by twelve noon Saturday." Enforceable also means that you must be present to ensure that the task is carried out. This means that for a rule to be most effective, a parent must be present to enforce the rule consistently.

Stating a Rule Positively
An effective rule needs to be worded positively. A positively worded rule communicates the idea that "First you work, then you play." ("Play" means any positive consequence.) For example, "Once you have cleaned your room, you may play outside." Another example: "After you eat your dinner, you may have dessert." Using *once* or *after* in stating the rule conveys the attitude that you expect the child to comply.

The following are examples of positively stated rules:

- "Once you have cleaned your room Saturday morning, you may go out and play."
- "You will receive your paycheck after you work your forty-hour week."

- "Eat your vegetables, and then you can have some pie."
- "As long as you maintain a B average at school, you may keep your part-time job."
- "After you mow the lawn, you may use the car."

Deductive Exercise

The leader says to the group, "Take five minutes to write down a rule you would like to implement with one of your children. Ask yourself if it is definable, reasonable, and enforceable. Please get in pairs, and for fifteen minutes help each other write an effective rule that meets our criteria."

Get responses from participants about the rule they will implement and focus on the three criteria for a rule.

Stage 5—Transition

The leader says to the group, "Please implement the rule you have chosen with one of your children this week, and next week we will discuss how things went implementing your rule with your child."

CHAPTER 6

WORKING WITH A CO-LEADER

As stated earlier, we strongly recommend that groups be co-led, that is, that two people plan and facilitate the group. I recognize that it may not be possible in many settings to free up two people to lead a group. Though worth the time and effort, utilizing this approach takes energy when the group meets and considerable planning before the group sessions occur. Having someone to share in the process can be fun and edifying for leaders and participants alike.

Co-leading is important for the ongoing growth and improvement of leadership skills. Co-leaders will plan together and give feedback and support to each other. If you are planning to co-lead your groups, here are some principles to follow with your co-leader.

Overall Perspective
Before your series of sessions begins, brainstorm everything that you think you would like to include in the x number of sessions. This is subject to change, depending on how fast your group proceeds. It is easy to lose sight of all that needs to be included in the course when you are in the process of leading the group, particularly when a point is exciting to the group or hard to understand. It helps to have an overall perspective written down before you begin the sessions so that you can realistically plan how much time needs to be spent on each topic.

Take notes on your plans for the sessions and save them so that you can refer to them to plan for subsequent groups. You think you will remember, but most likely you won't.

Set aside some time with your co-leader to plan each week for the session that week. Although you've made an overall plan for the x number of sessions your group will meet, do not try to make a detailed plan for more than one session at a time. There is no way to predict whether the group will understand or fail to understand what you present.

Divide Responsibilities

Though each of you needs to have input into the entire agenda for each session, divide responsibility for who will present what during the session. Make sure each leader has approximately the same amount of "on" time.

You need to meet with your co-leader *in person*. It won't work to plan via email or text. Both of you need to have input and awareness of every stage of the agenda, even those sections you are not presenting. Do not think you can divide up the agenda by simply assigning different parts of the session to each other without both leaders knowing the content of each part of the session.

I once knew co-leaders, Shelly and Tom, who led a group for seniors on preventive healthcare. Instead of following the recommended approach for co-leaders to meet in person to plan a session and to make sure each leader knows the content of what each is doing, Shelly and Tom assigned each other the different parts of the agenda for their class each session.

Midway through their six week class, Shelly got a call from Tom's partner telling her that Tom had been in a car accident and had broken his leg and was not meeting the group that evening, leaving Shelly to teach the entire session. Since Tom and Shelly had simply divided up the agenda for each session, Shelly didn't know the content of Tom's part of the session. Though participants were a bit confused, Shelly ended up shortening the class that evening to one hour instead of the usual two and presented only her part of the session.

Assign Time

Set up your sessions according to time. Anyone who has seen the curricula I have written knows that I indicate exactly how much time (to the best of my ability) a particular segment will take. Doing this will keep you on track and will dictate the modality you will use. It indicates the "weight" you give to a given topic. For example:

9:00–9:15—Opener

9:15–9:50—Exercise on consistency

9:50–10:15—Group discussion on consistency

Develop Materials

Decide if there are materials that need to be passed out or developed (PowerPoint presentations, handouts.)

Plan more than you can fit into the session (e.g., plan for two and a half hours if your group meets for two hours) to take care of the common worst-case scenario of *What will I do if I've presented everything and no one talks and I have an hour left in the session?* By the way, the opposite usually happens, that is, you do not have enough time to cover everything that you have planned.

Give Support and Feedback

Be honest and open with each other. Co-leading can be a source of joy and learning if the relationship between partners is an open one. You are models for your group. If there is anything uneasy between the two of you, the group more than likely will pick this up. Take the time to take care of little disturbances when they occur, and work through them with your co-leader before you meet your group.

Really listen to your co-leader. His ideas on, for example, criteria for choosing students for scholarships, might be very different from yours. Let him have space to share where he is on the subject. Active listening is an effective technique to use in a situation like this.

You do not have to present a "united front" to the group. The two of you might approach the theory of the course in a different way. You do not have to agree with each other on the "best" approach. Allow space for both of you to present your viewpoints to the group, recognizing the validity of each other's position. An attitude that is effective in the group is "Here's another approach to the same idea." One approach might click for some people and not for others.

Debrief Each Session

Debrief as soon after the end of each session as possible. A format for debriefing that has been constructive, growth-producing, and expedient (in terms of focusing) is to discuss highs, lows, and suggestions. Because reflection is an important component of this approach to learning, I often use this way of debriefing with a variety of groups.

Highs

Start the debriefing with the high points of that session—anything that pleased you during that time. Share these, both leaders adding what they consider to be high points. The high points might include what happened in the session in terms of how the group reacted, a comment from an individual, how you presented information, your (coleaders') interaction or reactions to each other, or how good the coffee was—*anything* that happened during the time your group was meeting that was positive.

Lows

After you have discussed the highs, share the low points that occurred in the group. Do not criticize your co-leader. During this part of the debriefing, focus on the group process or environmental issues such as "It was too hot in the room."

Suggestions

If you would have preferred the session to go differently, here's your chance to make an I-statement about how you feel. Examples of this type of I-statement are as follows:

- "I wonder what it would have been like if we had used a different exercise?"
- "I'm not comfortable with such-and-such exercise."
- "I'd like to start the class on time for the next session."

SECTION II:
FACILITATING SKILLS

CHAPTER 7
FACILITATING SKILLS TO MAXIMIZE LEARNING

You've scheduled your group, and you know the number of people attending. You're probably excited. You know that the Group Process Formula establishes a structure for the group that encourages the self-discovery of each participant and the growth of the group as a whole. But how do you respond to participants' comments and questions in an edifying way, and how do you forestall unhelpful behaviors in participants? How do you facilitate the group to maximize learning and make sure the group develops in a healthy way? We recommend the facilitating techniques discussed in this section in the following chapters.

In this part of the book, we present techniques for facilitating the group, providing concrete skills for listening to encourage participants' self-discovery and integration of skills. We also present methods for changing the direction of the group or the direction of a particular participant and introduce the importance to group leaders of recognizing and responding to nonverbal behaviors.

Real communication is very hard to achieve, but is essential for any leader. Some of us on occasion might judge, evaluate, approve, or disapprove before we really understand what the other person is saying and before we understand the frame of reference the other person is using. This tendency of most humans to react first by forming an evaluation of what has just been said and to evaluate it from our own point of view can be a barrier to mutual interpersonal communication and productive group facilitation.

Progress toward understanding can be made when this evaluative tendency is avoided, when we listen with understanding to participants, and when we actively listen to what is being said. This means that we need to see the expressed idea and attitudes from the other person's point of view, to sense how things feel to him, and to perceive his frame of reference in regard to the topic he is talking about. This is essential for group leaders. This is not simple to do and, for most of us, requires concentration.

Throughout your group sessions, you will be making decisions about whether to draw out a participant so that he keeps talking or clarifies his thinking, or not to draw him out and switch directions or move on. Most of the time, facilitating leaders listen and encourage participants to talk and participate. That is, as group leaders we *listen so people talk*.

Truly listening generously and effectively is an essential skill for leaders to master. We will describe in detail several techniques for listening: asking clarifying questions, paraphrasing, and actively listening, which are all essential skills for effective group facilitation.

There are, however, times when as a leader you want a participant to stop monopolizing the time, to stop playing games, to get "unstuck," or to stay on topic. When that is the situation, facilitating leaders need to employ skills that do not draw the participant out, but rather correct or change the direction the group is going. That is, you need to *talk so people listen* and express your needs or feelings firmly and sensitively so that people change their behavior. This is also important for effectively facilitating groups.

The skills for that purpose are very different from drawing out a member of the group. We recommend utilizing the skill of I-messages, which is simply expressing your needs to another person and identifying your feelings while being sensitive to the effect you have on the other person.

In the chapters that follow, we introduce concrete approaches in each category—listening skills to encourage people to talk and confronting skills so that the direction the group or a participant is going changes because of what we've said.

To be an effective leader who is maximizing the potential of the participants in your group, it is important to make sure you have facility with skills for both occurrences and know when to utilize those skills.

CHAPTER 8

LISTENING SO PEOPLE TALK

Listening is part of our everyday life, and all of us have had experience with people who *really* listen. It might be hard to put your finger on what exactly that good listener did to make you feel heard. It can be one of those situations where "I know it when I see (experience) it." My hunch is that you like being with good listeners. I've not encountered anyone who has said, "I don't like being with Fred because he's such a good listener." Most often when we are with someone who is genuinely listening, it sends the message that the listener is truly interested in what we are saying and in us.

The skills associated with effective and generous listening are the foundation for good group facilitation. In this chapter, we have delineated several techniques for good listening. As is the case with any skill, the more you practice these techniques, the better you will be at employing them and recognizing situations when just listening (not advising or suggesting) is the best approach.

In this chapter, we will discuss techniques for listening so participants in our groups are more prone to talk. We will present six specific techniques we can use to listen so that participants can explore how the information presented in the group fits into their lives and so we can encourage them to integrate these concrete skills to change their lives for the better.

Silence

Silence is a way of listening that encourages a participant to talk because you are respectfully waiting for her to proceed. Silence as we are defining it is not just being quiet, but calmly and attentively not saying anything to give the group member time and space to think. This type of silence builds trust.

Being silent is extremely difficult when you are a leader of a group. We want to fill in the silences because silence makes us, and often others, uncomfortable. People in our groups need the space and time to think about the material we have presented so they can work through their own process of self-discovery. Being silent can send the message that as the leader you know that the participant needs to figure out how the information fits for him—that he has the answers for his life.

Utilizing silence is important for facilitating leaders, but too often silence is not used. When you ask a question and get silence in response, you might want to reword the question or explain what you mean. Unless someone is really confused, don't say anything. Be silent. Participants need time to think about what you have said. Being silent can build trust with your participants. They know that you are not going to rush them without letting them think about what has been said.

Silence also raises anxiety, so most often *someone* (a participant, that is) will break the silence. Just make sure that *you're* not the one to break the silence. If you feel the need to do so, start counting silently to one hundred, or count the hairs on the participant's head—anything to make sure you don't jump in.

Door Openers

Door openers are invitations to participants to say more. They open the door for the person to continue if he wants to. Door openers can be received very differently from a question such as, "What do you mean?" which the participant may feel is "pointed." Using door openers is a *gentle* way to encourage more information from the group member. Door openers do not communicate a judgmental response to what has been said, but most often are neutral responses from the facilitator that send the message, *Please continue.*

Here are some door openers you might use:

- "Oh."
- "Uh-huh."
- "Interesting."
- "You did, eh?"
- "I'd like to hear more."
- "I can tell you feel very strongly about that."
- "You looked like you were going to say something."
- "I see."
- "Really?"
- "Tell me more about that."
- "Describe what that was like for you."
- "I'd be interested in hearing more."

Clarifying Questions

Think Deeper

Because you want the participant to solve her own problem, which will increase her confidence, your questions need to be ones that make her think more deeply about the issue presented. Clarifying questions are worded to minimize the receiver's only responding with a yes or a no answer. For example, asking a participant if he had seen a particular behavior in his teenager before, would most likely elicit a yes or no answer. Asking him, rather, to describe the behavior he would like to see in his teen would encourage him to think about and describe what he would like to see. Clarifying questions are used to invite the participant to say more in a descriptive way and can help the leader understand more clearly the situation or point of view of the participant and help the group member sort through his own thinking.

The Key—"You"

The word *you* needs to be a part of every clarifying question since the responses are specific to the person's individual life. The "you" really means "for your life." A question like, "What are characteristics of exceptional leaders?" is not a clarifying question, but a question like, "What do *you* think are characteristics of exceptional leaders?" is a clarifying question. Using the word *you* in this way helps the participant think about what the question means for him and not how he feels in general about the content of the question.

Suspend Your Goal

The person asking the question, the leader of the group, does not have an expectation or goal in terms of an action or direction in mind for a member of the group. The purpose of clarifying questions is not to gather facts or information. Sometimes what the participant is saying may not be clear to you. If it seems clear to him, let it go.

The focus needs to stay with the individual, and stopping his thinking to get you up to speed might interrupt that process. Asking, "You don't want your project manager to quit, do you, by taking that approach?" is not a clarifying question because it would elicit a yes or no. Such a question probably reflects the questioner's bias or point of view rather than helps the participant clarify his thinking.

No Statement behind the Question

Clarifying questions do not have a statement behind them. For example, "Do you really believe that?" is a question with a statement behind it (though it contains the word "you") which might be, "I don't believe that." Clarifying questions do not imply judgment (either positive or negative).

With clarifying questions, we are asking the person to think and explore more deeply, and we are giving her the space to do so. With our questions, we are pushing the limits gently.

Here are some examples of clarifying questions:

- "What might you do differently next time?"
- "What are your options for _____?"
- "What was it like for you when _____?"
- "What are some alternatives you've considered?"
- "How did you feel about that?"
- "How did that work for you?"

Extensions

Extensions again are invitations to the participant to say more. They can be quite effective in helping the learner extend the thought or idea that he has just expressed.

Here are some examples of extensions:

- You repeat the end of his or her sentence: for example "Trouble with your boss…?"
- You ask, "If you did that, then what would happen?"
- You say, "Your worst fantasy about that is …?"
- You re-create with elaborate description the scene the participant has just shared. For example, you say to a participant, "When you walked into the house and got dinner ready, and all of you sat down, and then Sally, your three-year-old, picked up food to throw it, you …?"

Paraphrasing

Feedback

How do you check to make sure that you understand the other person's ideas, information, or suggestions as she intended them? How do you know that her remark means the same to you as it does to her?

Paraphrasing is a form of feedback. Paraphrasing is stating *in your own words* what another's remarks mean to you. This, then, gives the other person the opportunity to determine whether her message is coming across as she intended.

Paraphrasing can be used to show participants in a group what the individual's idea or suggestion means to you. As group leaders, we utilize paraphrasing when we want to demonstrate that we are interested in what the other person has to say and sometimes to clarify the participant's statement if it seems unclear.

Understanding the Facts

Many of us use paraphrasing quite effectively. It simply is saying in other words what the participant has said. We are feeding back to the participant the facts of what she has said in our own words. This lets the group member know that we have heard and understood what he has said.

Take the following for example:

> PARTICIPANT "I can't do anything with my child when my mother-in-law is around. I tell him not to eat candy, but she gives him candy."

> FACILITATOR "It's difficult for you to discipline your son when your mother-in-law is present because she undermines what you want."

Interest

An additional benefit of paraphrasing is that it lets the other person know that you are interested in him. It is evidence that you do want to understand what he means. The act of paraphrasing itself conveys interest in the other and expresses your concern to see how he views things.

If you state in your own way what his remark conveys to you, then the other person can begin to determine whether his message is coming through as he intended. Then, if he thinks you have misunderstood, he can speak directly to the specific misunderstanding you have stated.

Word Swapping

Paraphrasing is not word swapping or parroting, that is, just saying what the other has said in different words. People sometimes think of paraphrasing as merely expressing the other person's words in another way. Take the following for example:

> SARAH "Jim should not be a teacher."
>
> FRED "You mean Jim really shouldn't be teaching?"
>
> SARAH "I'm not sure."

Instead of saying something like that, paraphrase by asking yourself, What does what the other said mean to me?" and feeding that back to the participant.

> SARAH "Jim should not be a teacher."
>
> FRED "You mean he doesn't like kids?"
>
> SARAH "Oh, no. I mean that he has such expensive tastes that I'm afraid he'll never earn enough to have the lifestyle he wants by being a teacher."

FRED "You think he should have gone into a different profession that would have ensured him a higher standard of living?"

SARAH "Exactly!"

Active Listening[3]

Identifying Feelings
I have always had an interest in the characteristics and traits exceptional leaders demonstrate and have recently launched a project where I interview leaders and simply ask them their take on leadership. I have had the privilege of interviewing CEOs of corporations, unrecognized lay leaders, executive directors of nonprofit organizations, presidents of foundations, and retired community organizers. Of the two dozen people I have interviewed so far, all have stated that the most important skill good leaders have *is the ability to listen deeply* and with empathy. That is not easy to achieve, but it is essential for effective leadership.

All too often we have the feeling of not being heard, of not being understood. And sometimes we don't understand ourselves, though we have a sense that something is going on with us on a level that we cannot quite figure out.

Others might accuse us of not listening or of rushing in too quickly with an answer, a suggestion, an example from our own life, or a piece of advice. Although we might not be comfortable in situations where we refrain from giving advice quickly or where our advice may appear to be off target, we may not know of another way to truly help another person.

---

[3] I have described the communication skills in my own words based on what I have learned from using and teaching the skills. The inspiration for some of the listening and speaking skills came from Dr. Thomas Gordon's *Effectiveness Training series*,1980.

Active listening is a skill that goes deeper than paraphrasing because the focus is not only on the facts of what the person is communicating but is also, and more importantly, on the feeling she is conveying. As the listener, you are identifying the feeling you think the other is experiencing, whether she has identified that feeling or not.

Maximizing Skills Integration

In everyday communication, responding to the facts of what a person communicates is most often the appropriate response. It helps you to clarify what the other has said. However, sometimes we need to listen and respond to the feelings the person is sending as well in order to help him. For group leaders and change makers, the skill of active listening can make a significant difference in maximizing participants' ability to integrate skills to change their lives for the better.

Active listening is not a skill for solving problems or even coming to a decision, though that may happen and actually often does happen. We often want to "tie it with a bow" – to make sure there is a solution. When we are listening and not pushing the participant toward a decision or solution, we are sending the message that we believe the answers to the issue lie within the participant. *This attitude and belief on the part of the facilitator undergirds autonomy and confidence in the participant.*

We all know that some decisions don't come quickly and might take days, weeks, or even more time to be made. Active listening can facilitate participants' self-discovery, thereby enabling them to make the best decisions for their lives.

Unexpressed Feelings

Active listening is one of the most powerful skills we can employ when we are genuinely trying to help another. To actively listen is to hear not only what is said, but also what is possibly unsaid. This communication skill opens up the possibility for increasing the depth of the communication that takes place between individuals and for strengthening the relationship between people who care about one another. Active listening can lower another's emotional temperature. And as the listener, you may act as a sounding board for the other person.

When active listening is utilized, the sender and the listener often feel warmth and intimacy. The skill of active listening is a powerful one both for the listener and the sender. It most often results in a sense of really being heard.

Making an Educated Guess
Active listening means identifying the feeling beneath what the participant has said and sending the message back to him with a questioning inflection since it is an educated guess on your part.

Following is an example of active listening:

> COLLEAGUE "I don't think I can continue working here."
>
> YOU "You're worried that your skills and training don't fit?"
>
> COLLEAGUE "No. I have trouble with Jodie, my boss."
>
> YOU "It frustrates you because you and your boss clash?"
>
> COLLEAGUE "Look, I'm good at my job. I know more than she does, but she's always looking over my shoulder."
>
> YOU "That makes you angry!"
>
> COLLEAGUE "Sure does. I just can't work like that, being micromanaged every minute."

What Is the Purpose of Active Listening?

To Maximize Self-Discovery
Active listening serves many purposes. As group leaders we utilize it to help participants clarify their thinking and maximize their own self-discovery. With active listening, we make sure the spotlight is totally on the person speaking. It fosters in-depth communication, not just superficial communication, which can result in new insights and awareness in the participant.

To Vent
As facilitators, we want to make sure we've heard the participant correctly, and with active listening we show the group member we are genuinely interested in her as a person. Sometimes participants need to vent about their work situation, their children, or their colleagues in order to truly take in new information. Active listening can help with their identifying those feelings and putting them aside to let in new information.

We use active listening when another person has a strong feeling or a problem and when the other needs time and space to focus on his thoughts and feelings. Active listening provides feedback to the person and helps him come to the decision or solution that is best for him. It also provides time for the person to sort through ideas and feelings or perhaps just vent.

To Encourage Mastery
At the core of good facilitation is the belief that participants really do have the answers to their problems or issues within themselves. Active listening is a skill facilitators can use to increase participants' self-awareness, encourage independence, and help them problem-solve.

In our groups there are no favorites, star students, or monopolizers. As facilitators of learning and change, we want each member of the group to know he is important. Active listening helps foster meaningful levels of interaction so that each person feels important and heard.

Active Listening Starters

For most of us, it's hard to identify other people's feelings, and it feels weird to send that feeling back to them, even if it's just an educated guess. What if they get mad? Or what if you identify an incorrect feeling or they think you are trying to psychoanalyze them? If you are truly and genuinely actively listening and you care about the other person, most likely those worst-case scenarios won't materialize. But as is the case with any skill, the more you practice, the better you will get.

Try out active listening and see how it feels for you. To minimize the risk that might accompany active listening some people, I encourage people initially to actively listen to strangers, for example, the checkout clerk at the grocery store (who'll love you for your interest!) or the man sitting next to you on your flight to Chicago, or the barista at Starbucks making your latte.

There are a variety of ways to start an active listening response to help you sound less stilted and repetitive. Following are some active listening starters (the underlined feeling word will change depending on what you've heard):

- o "I see. You mean that you <u>hoped</u> she would …"
- o "It sounds to me like you're <u>sad</u> about …"
- o "Sounds like you're <u>excited</u> about …"
- o "You feel <u>upset</u> about …"
- o "You're feeling it's <u>unfair</u> that …"
- o "You mean you're <u>afraid</u> of …"
- o "You sound like you feel <u>anxious</u> about …"
- o "You look <u>worried</u> about …"
- o "I'm not sure I understand. Do you mean you're <u>disappointed</u> that …"
- o "You <u>hate</u> that …"
- o "You're <u>confused</u> about …"
- o "You're really <u>clear</u> about that. Your mother …"
- o "You <u>hate</u> it when I refuse to give you an answer."

- o "You feel <u>lonely</u> right now because …"
- o "You <u>wish</u> Tommy would …"
- o "You're <u>upset</u> with your mother because …"
- o "You're <u>irritated</u> with me because …"
- o "I think I understand. You're (feeling word). Is that it?"
- o "I bet that's <u>frustrating</u>."
- o "Are you saying you're so <u>frustrated</u> that you …?"
- o "You seem <u>disturbed</u> about …"
- o "I hear you saying you're <u>unhappy</u> with …"
- o "It's <u>embarrassing</u> for you to …"
- o "It seems <u>unfair</u> to you that …"
- o "It's <u>frightening</u> to …"
- o "It's totally <u>hopeless</u> right now?"
- o "It <u>hurts</u> when you …"
- o "That's really <u>important</u> to you. You want …"
- o "Wow! That makes you feel <u>proud</u> about …"
- o "That makes you feel <u>left out</u> when …"
- o "When that happens, you feel <u>resentful</u>."

Key Points

- Silence can build trust.
- We can listen to the facts another person is saying and feed them back to him by using paraphrasing.
- Active listening is the most powerful listening skill.
- Active listening provides feedback.
- Active listening is not a skill for solving the sender's problem, or even for coming to a decision, though that may happen.
- Active listening proves to the sender that not only have you heard her, but also you have understood. Understanding does not necessarily mean agreeing with.
- It shows the sender that you are interested in her as a person.
- Active listening gives the sender a chance to vent. Feelings can be fleeting.
- It communicates acceptance of the sender. Acceptance of the sender is different from accepting what she says.
- Active listening fosters the other's doing his own problem-defining and problem-solving. He holds onto the ball.
- It fosters the sender's moving from a superficial to a deeper, more basic level.
- Active listening fosters the sender's ability to deal with feelings, not just with facts.

CHAPTER 9

TALKING SO PEOPLE LISTEN

As facilitating leaders, we are most often in a helping relationship with participants, that is, we are listening so people talk. We know that feelings are an important influencing factor in human communication, and that active listening is a particularly powerful skill for responding to the feelings behind another person's message in a way that would maximize keeping communication open. The flip side of this is when we need to *talk so a person listens*.

Sometimes as group facilitators we don't want a participant to continue talking because he might be off track, we think what he's saying isn't appropriate or productive, or we're concerned about not getting to important information because of the time the participant is taking. You don't want to draw that participant out or encourage him to continue. You want to stop the participant and change the direction of the group or the thinking of that particular group member. When this occurs you want to talk so people listen.

In this chapter, we will discuss four techniques for confronting group members or changing the direction of the group that minimize hard feelings on the part of the participant.

Throw It Back to the Individual

Sometimes you may feel like you are getting nowhere, that everything you say or that another participant contributes, is met with some kind of roadblock from another group member. Suggestions are rejected by the member, or what he is saying seems confusing to you and other participants. If this occurs, you might want to throw it back to the participant instead of making suggestions that are rejected. This way you keep the ball in his court and send the message that he is the one who has the answers within himself.

Here are some phrases and questions that you might want to use in this type of situation:

- "What would you like to have happen?"
- "Would you like to get some ideas about that?"
- "I'm not clear about what the problem is."

Brainstorming

Sometimes members of the group are genuinely stuck and would benefit from help in getting themselves unstuck to expand their ideas or broaden their perspective. A technique you might want to employ in that case is brainstorming. The purpose of brainstorming is to generate a lot of ideas when someone is stuck.

As the facilitator, ask the stuck participant if she would like to hear some ideas from the group. If she's willing, tell the group that certain rules will be followed while you're brainstorming:

"We want as many ideas as possible. At this point quantity is more important than quality, so throw into the ring anything that comes to mind. Also, we're not going to judge the ideas at all, neither positively or negatively—no commenting whatsoever."

"Susie can write down the ideas if she wants to and decide for herself what fits best for her situation. We'll take the next five minutes to brainstorm ideas for Susie's situation."

Ask Susie to take a minute to review her situation before the group starts brainstorming.

Tactful Shifts

We use tactful shifts by reinforcing what the participant is saying or doing that is positive and then adding or stopping what we don't want to see continue. Effective group leaders employ the technique of tactful shifts often in their groups.

Following are some examples of tactful shifts you might want to use in your groups:

- "I can see you have strong feelings about that. We need to move on."
- "You have strong feelings about that. I wonder how it relates to _____?"
- "We will talk about that next week. Can you hold on to that question until then?"
- "I'm not sure we can help you here with that. Maybe we could talk after class about some alternatives for you."
- "That may work. For the purposes of this class, we want you to try _____."

I-Messages

With I-messages, we need to state our wants and needs in a way that maximizes the other's reciprocal response with minimal damage to the relationship. This is true in our day-to-day encounters with friends, family, or colleagues and also when we are in a group setting.

I-messages are sentences utilizing the word *I* plus your feeling or need. It sounds simple to make an I-statement, but it can be difficult. With I-messages you don't usually tell the other person what to do to correct the situation, nor do you use judgmental words or phrases.

Sometimes, however, we need to confront someone regarding an issue or problem we have with his behavior. An I-message can help us deliver our message to another person with minimum damage to the relationship. When we utilize the skill of I-messages, we express ourselves to others, identifying our feelings or needs while being sensitive to the effect we are having on the other person. With I-messages we hope to bring about a change in the behavior of the other person. To confront another with the negative feelings evoked by his or her behavior can be risky. To do so in a way that entails minimal risk to the relationship, however, is a skill that can be learned.

When people express negative feelings about another's behavior, they may do so in a way that might hurt or anger the other. For example, "I can't believe you're so unaware that I clean up every evening or what time it is!" Our words may damage the relationship. In those cases often the message that was meant to be heard may be sharply ignored, which is different from saying, "I need to get downtown in a half hour. Would you please put the dishes in the dishwasher tonight?"

Using the word *I* plus stating your need or feeling can increase the *likelihood* that the other person will change his behavior. With I-messages, "I" take a risk. The other person might say, "Oh, okay." The response also might be, "What the hell?" When this happens, clearly the other has strong feelings, brought on by your I-message. Since his feelings are strong, actively listen as he expresses those strong feelings. When you want the other person to change in a specific way, make sure you state that clearly.

Here are some examples of I-messages:

- "I sense your confusion."
- "I'm concerned about the time."
- "In the interest of time, I need to move on."
- "I'm concerned that you are overwhelmed."
- "I will need to get that information for you."
- "That's not been my experience."

I-Message Situations

Not all sentences with the word *I* in them are I-messages, and not all I-messages have the word *I* in them. Choose the response for each of the following situations that you think is the best I-message.

Situation 1: You are talking on the phone to a friend, getting directions to the neighborhood picnic. Your three children are noisy and distracting.

Your response to your children is:

    A. "I wish all of you could keep your mouths closed just once."
    B. "I would like for you to behave yourselves."
    C. "Hey, I can't hear what Mary is saying."

Situation 2: At a board meeting, one of the members continues to talk over other members. You find yourself more and more irritated by the behavior.

You respond to the situation by saying:

    A. "Bill, I would appreciate it if you would stop interrupting so much."
    B. "I am having a hard time hearing what Harry is saying when more than one person is talking at once."
    C. "I think, Bill, that you act very well sometimes and very poorly at other times."

Situation 3: Your child, you feel, is deliberately dawdling so that he will miss the bus and you will drive him to school. You resent being a chauffeur.

You say to him:

    A. "Get your tail end moving."

B. "I'm not going to drive you to school."
C. "It irritates me that you are not ready for school, and I'm afraid you'll miss your bus."

Situation 4: You are at a play, and the man in front of you is wearing a hat that is preventing you from seeing anything. What do you say to him?

Here are some possibilities for Situation 4:

> "Excuse me, I'm not able to see the stage." (Then hope he takes the hint.)

> or

> "I'm eager to see the play, but I am not able to. Would you mind taking your hat off?"

Answer Key: 1 – C; 2 – B; 3 – C

Key Points

- With I-messages, "I" take a risk.
- Tactful shifts reinforce what is positive about what a participant is doing and also makes the shift you want to see.
- There's no guarantee that I-messages will change the other person's behavior, but they do maximize that possibility.

In Summary

When you want to listen to the facts, use paraphrasing or clarifying questions.

When you want to listen to the feelings, use the following:

- active listening
- clarifying questions
- silence
- door openers

When you want to listen for the purpose of your own clarification, use the following:

- paraphrasing
- active listening
- clarifying questions
- extensions
- I-messages

When you want to listen to facilitate a decision, use the following:

- clarifying questions
- active listening
- extensions

CHAPTER 10

ROADBLOCKS TO EFFECTIVE COMMUNICATION

As group leaders, we can sabotage our best efforts because we fail to effectively communicate. In traditional teaching and learning settings, the students look to the leader or teacher for the answers and value his or her advice and suggestions. Most often the advice can be valuable and just what the student was seeking. That paradigm is different from what we as effective group facilitators want to do for our participants. Our role is to assist each participant on her journey of self-discovery and to help her integrate newfound skills that make sense for her everyday life.

Sometimes our responses to members of our groups stop the flow of communication; sometimes they do not. As group facilitators we need to be aware of the possibility of the following as roadblocks, particularly when we really want to listen to what the other is saying.

There are three categories of roadblocks: **rescuing**, which is basically telling the other person what to do; **insisting**, which is when you see something the other person doesn't and you encourage or even demand he or she sees the situation your way; and **not accepting**, which means that you judge the person and/or what he is saying.

Rescuing

When you are rescuing a participant, you basically are telling him what to do rather than helping him come to his own conclusions. Usually when the rescuing roadblocks occur, particularly with giving advice and suggesting solutions, it is because the person to whom you're giving the advice is not there yet. You might see the obvious solution, but she does not and therefore finds it hard to hear what you are suggesting.

When you hear a participant say any form of "Yes, but …," what you have said is a roadblock to good communication. Offering solutions and giving advice does not always serve as a roadblock to communication, but sometimes it does. As leaders, we need to know when these responses are effective and when they serve as roadblocks.

Here are examples of ways people can "rescue" others and therefore set up a roadblock to productive communication:

- **Ordering or directing** (no one likes to be told what to do)
  - "Just tell your husband he has to help you raise those children."
  - "If you are in that much pain, go to a doctor."
- **Advising, giving suggestions, or offering solutions** (an invitation to "Yes, but …")
  - "Why don't you try talking it over with Sally?"
  - "Have you talked to your boss about the problem?"
  - "I think it's time you see a lawyer."
- **Interpreting, analyzing, or diagnosing**
  - "Probably because you don't have a big staff, you don't understand the situation."
  - "Freddie gets away with murder in your class!"
- **Probing and questioning**
  - "When did you start feeling this way?"
  - "How long will you let the situation go on like that?"
  - "Why did you react that way to your boss?"

Insisting

It can be frustrating when participants don't get what we are saying or don't buy it. As leaders, we might subtly or not so subtly employ techniques that insist that group members do in fact believe what we are saying and eventually use the information. After all, we're the ones with more knowledge about the subject matter than anyone else in the room. Ha!

Here are some ways we might *insist* participants see things our way:

- o **Moralizing or preaching**
  - ▪ "It damages people's self-esteem when they are yelled at."
  - ▪ "Everyone loves to be complimented."
  - ▪ "You certainly can confront him with your feelings."
  - ▪ "You'll feel better, and he'll respect you in the long run."
- o **Logical arguments**
  - ▪ "College can be the best years of your life."
  - ▪ "If you want her to listen to you, you'll have to listen to her."
- o **Labeling, stereotyping, or assuming**
  - ▪ "Women have more responsibility for raising children than men do."
  - ▪ "How many of you men really enjoy cooking?"
  - ▪ "The employees who are not doing well are probably the ones who didn't take the training."

Not Accepting

At times it can be difficult to understand where a participant is along his journey of self-discovery. It is particularly difficult to accept a participant where he is if it is clear that he is hurting. We want to make it better—and his pain might very well make us uncomfortable. When this happens, we might employ responses that send the message that we do not accept where the member of the group really is. In that case, our communication most likely will be a roadblock. For example, a downtrodden member of your group might say, "I'm really not very good at my job." If you were to send a nonaccepting roadblock, you might say, "I don't think you're bad at your job. I've heard a lot of good things about your work."

Although you might respond to the participant with all good intentions of reassuring him, and although you may sincerely believe what you are saying, it does not address where the participant is, so your good intentions of reassuring him will probably fall on deaf ears.

Here are ways people communicate when they are *not accepting* of where another is at the time:

- o **Reassuring or sympathizing**
  - "You'll feel better in the morning."
  - "I know just how you feel."
  - "Things will work out well for you when you are transferred to a different department."
- o **Praising**
  - "But you're doing so well with following through."
  - "Oh, I think you are a good mother."
- o **Withdrawing or diverting**
  - "Look, just don't worry about it."
  - "This isn't the time to talk about that."
  - "Yes, well, let's move on to something else."
- o **Judging**
  - "You don't really want to do such a horrible thing to your employees, do you?"
  - "That's a lousy idea."

CHAPTER 11

NONVERBAL BEHAVIOR

We all communicate nonverbally—with our hands, eyebrows, mouth, tone of voice, and inflection—all the time whether we are speaking or listening. As a facilitating leader, it is important to be aware of nonverbal behaviors exhibited by participants in your group. Nonverbal behavior, sometimes called body language, includes facial expression, gestures, body posture, and glances—any gesture that a person makes either while talking or not talking. Nonverbal behavior can express our feelings about what we are saying or what we are not saying.

Most of us have seen the following and have "gotten the message":

- someone pacing up and down in a hospital waiting room
- a person slouching in a chair and not making eye contact with anyone
- a child looking frightened
- an employee with his eyes on the ceiling while scratching his head
- a third grade teacher wagging her finger with one hand on her hip
- a woman with her arms outstretched and a big grin on her face

If we were to add words to one of the foregoing examples, like for the woman with her arms outstretched, she might say, "Honey, you're home at last!" We would recognize that her verbal and nonverbal behaviors make sense or are *congruent*—that is, they match.

Sometimes in communication, however, a problem arises when our words don't match what is going on on our face, in our gestures, or with our tone of voice. When the verbal and nonverbal communication do not match, when it is *incongruent,* we most often respond to (or "buy") the message the person is sending with her nonverbal behavior, not her verbal expression.

This incongruent communication style can make us feel confused, mistrustful, angry, or uneasy about the person who is sending the message.

For example, someone might say the following while doing something incongruent:

- "I am listening to what you are saying!" (He is saying this while looking down at his cell phone.)
- "Well, you went and did it again!" (Then the person laughs or chuckles and looks delighted.)
- "Yeah, I'd really like to do that." (The person is frowning and looking doubtful.)
- "I really feel down today." (The person is grinning and shaking his head.)
- "My toddlers are so bad!" (The person is grinning and her eyes are dancing.)
- "All right, if that's what you want to do." (The person has his arms folded across his chest and has turned away.)
- "That's all right. I don't mind." (The person's smile has a stiff, frozen appearance.)
- "I'm not angry." (Then the person walks away from you, goes into another room, and closes the door.)
- You ask your child what he's doing, and he says, "Oh nothing," but he looks like the cat that swallowed the canary.

When a message is incongruent, what do you experience? Do you buy what the other is saying? What is it exactly that makes you buy or not buy what the other is saying?

Most often we pick up on incongruity between what the person's words say and what his or her nonverbal expression is saying. You respond to this incongruity and may feel confused, uncomfortable, doubtful, resentful, tense, and/or unconvinced.

Even though we might have uneasy feelings when communication is incongruent, we might elect to only respond to what is said depending on the relationship we have with the sender. With friends and family we might respond with, "It doesn't look like that's what you want to do," which is an invitation for the other to tell you what's going on. Most often, whether we directly respond to it or not, the nonverbal behavior cancels out the verbal, though on the surface we may only respond to what the other person is saying.

As a facilitator of a group, when you see nonverbal behavior without words, it may be time for you to invite the member of the group to participate, for example, "Karen, it looks like you have a question" or "Fred, did I further confuse the situation?"

Key Points about Nonverbal Behavior

- It is impossible not to communicate. (Example: "I have sent you seven emails and have received no answer." The failure to respond is an answer.)
- The nonverbal message is the unspoken statement about the relationship between the two people who are communicating, including how one is experiencing oneself and/or the other at this point in time and at this point in the relationship.
- When a person's words are used to disguise rather than communicate, her voice, body language, and movements often give her away.
- What is not expressed openly seeks expression in other ways.
- Our nonverbal expressions are often more reflective of what we are really experiencing than our words are.
- When our nonverbals do not match the words we say, the nonverbals tend to cancel out or disqualify the verbal message.
- When there is incongruity between our verbal and nonverbal messages, the other person usually responds to the nonverbal message.

CHAPTER 12

ADDITIONAL TECHNIQUES FOR EFFECTIVE GROUP FACILITATION

Now you've learned how to draw out participants and how to help them switch gears and not continue what they are saying or doing. Included in this chapter are some additional tips to keep in mind for effective facilitation.

The following are some general ideas to make sure your facilitation is maximizing learning for your participants.

✓ Personal Examples

For a group leader, using your own personal examples can help the subject matter come alive for participants. Share with your groups your successes and your nonsuccesses. This sends the message that you are human, sometimes successful and sometimes not. What was it like for you to implement the skills you hope participants will use or the information you hope will raise their awareness? Your examples will stick with participants and may be the most powerful vehicle for their changing their behavior for the better.

You might want to share experiences with sentence stems like the following:

- "When my son was five, I _____."
- "I remember a participant who _____."
- "I'm reminded of a man in the leadership class who _____."
- "When I worked at my last job, I _____."

✓ Be a Storyteller

This is very similar to providing personal examples, except it usually takes a little longer. Stories, as opposed to personal examples, are often how we make sense of facts and convey to others who we are, what we value, and how we've dealt with challenges. Stories can communicate the idea to someone else that they're not alone and can be a way of encouraging others. They can serve as a vehicle for people to identify with the story and with the content you are communicating or teaching.

If you have stories from your life that will illuminate the points you hope to make with participants, by all means tell those stories. If you know of a story you've heard from a friend, colleague, or family member, or from something you've read, and if it clarifies the point you want to make, then tell the story to your group. Think of the stories you have heard that have really stuck with you and what they have taught you. Stories are a powerful teaching tool that often broaden our perspective. They are not used often enough.

✓ Don't Judge

To use this process most effectively, put aside the function of judge and do not feel compelled to decide whether an answer is good or bad / right or wrong. Try to avoid comments that imply either a positive or a negative reaction. Avoid "Good," "You don't mean that, do you?", "Fine," "Great," "That's right," and "That's not right, is it?"

✓ Encouraging Responses

Do use "thank you," "okay," and other nonjudgmental responses.

✓ Join In

Join in the group exercises and activities when appropriate. Delay your response or answer when you want to avoid the group's mirroring you. Share first when you want them to model your response.

✓ Making Mistakes

There is nothing wrong with going back when you feel you've bombed and saying, "Wait! Erase! Scratch what I just said." Start over with your I-message—"I made a mistake, and I'm uncomfortable with what I just said or did."

✓ Practice

The more you practice the skills, the easier it becomes to recognize when you are on target or off target.

✓ Accept

In the end, when you have tried everything with a particular participant, sometimes an alternative is to accept what you cannot change.

By acceptance, I do not mean resignation or agreeing with the other's perspective. The sense with acceptance in this occurrence is: *It's all right for you to feel the way you do, and it's all right for me to feel the way I do. I still don't agree with you. I will not give up or change my values, but I am comfortable with and accept you and your feelings.*

CHAPTER 13

TYING IT ALL TOGETHER

Please consider the following situations and decide what you would do if you were the facilitator of the group when the situation occurred. What would you say? What would you do?

What Would You Do If ...

- a participant refused to participate in an exercise?

- a participant accused you of something? (For example: "You talk about listening, but you haven't listened to me since the class began.")

- a participant started analyzing, putting down, or belittling another participant?

- a person said to you, "Don't you feel it's wrong to _____ (spank a child, excuse a fifteen-year-old from being late to class, praise employees for a job they should do anyway, etc.)?"

- a participant asked you what he or she could do about getting spouse, employee, or parent involved in your group because the person needs it badly?

- a participant said to you, "The reason you don't understand what it's like is because you are a man (or a woman, or middle class, or the boss). It's easy for you to dismiss what I'm saying"?

- a participant said, "I don't understand this material (or concept or idea). Please explain it again"? (the information is information you as a leader *also* do not understand.)

- a person said, "Abortion is bad and has nothing to do with this class. I don't know why you brought it up anyway. I'm here to get information about_____"?

- a participant said, "I don't buy what you're saying. You're not advocating _____, are you?"

- a participant said, "What you're saying would never work for me"?

- a participant refuses to "pair up" with another member of the group for the Opener"?

CHAPTER 14

HOOKS AND GAMES

It sometimes happens in groups that people play games in order to avoid taking action. We're asking members of our groups to change, and change is hard. It also happens that as group facilitators, we can get hooked by those game players and let them get us off target, away from what we had hoped to convey. We also might have experienced groups where the group leader was playing games and participants respond to those games. Again, the reason most often is to avoid changing.

I learned the concept of hooks and games from Bill Cornell, clinical psychologist, who now is well-known for his exceptional leadership in Transactional Analysis. A couple of decades ago Bill was my supervisor, friend, teacher, and confidant. His impact on my way of thinking and the trajectory of my lifework is profound. I am grateful for having learned from this exceptional human being, coach, and thinker.

Games Group Leaders Might Play

There are many ways to facilitate groups, and my hunch is that most of us have experienced group leaders who fit one or more of the following games group leaders might play. The descriptions are exaggerated to show the effect of group leadership styles and attitudes that we may have experienced (or assumed) at one time or another.

Helper
The attitude is this: *As a group leader, I'm here to tell you what you need to do in order to "cure" whatever your problem is. I have the answer, cure, or solution.* It's like the participant has a toothache and you're the dentist who is going to fix it. This group leader, teacher, or instructor always has *the* answer.

Garbage Collector—"Tell Me Everything That Is Wrong"
The attitude is this: *As a group we're here to complain, moan, and groan. As a group leader, I'm here to collect all your ills. Give me your garbage; put it in my bucket.* This often happens when the group is homogeneous—for example, a group of parents of teens, human resource directors from the same corporation, or second and third grade teachers from the same school.

Bartender
Sometimes participants get into a "I can top that" game or a bout of "Let's swap stories." They might say things like, "Well, I can top that!" or, "That's nothing. Listen to this." This can be fun, but it may mean that nobody gets anywhere, though some group leaders let this continue.

I Believe!
The group leader has the attitude of: *I'll read this material to you though some of it might not make sense to me or fit for you. I haven't really integrated it, but it must be important and must work because it's written here.*

I'm So Nice!
The group leader's motivation is: *These people* will *like me because I'm cute, nice, good, and/or entertaining, and I laugh a lot, praise them, love them, empathize with them, or do whatever they want. If it pleases the group members, fine. You (participant) be the leader.*

Guru
The group leader's attitude is: *You are lucky to have me as your teacher. I know from experience and training, and I know pretty much everything.*

Sit at my feet and learn. I am an authority on (behavior, communication, human resource development, parenting, tai chi, transcendental meditation, psychotherapy, marriage, values clarification—just fill in the blank).

To genuinely facilitate a group, assume this attitude: *This is a process. I'm here to provide information, support, and encouragement for participants so they can discover how to be more effective and happier. I am not here to solve problems. I am facilitating participants' solving their own problems.*

Getting "Hooked" as a Group Leader

Sometimes group leaders get off target and wonder how they got there. They might feel like the group, or even one participant, is running the group and that they've lost control. They may wonder why they think a participant is particularly irritating or why they dread calling on someone in the group. When this happens, you as a group leader are hooked. (Again, thanks to Bill Cornell.)

Group facilitators are hooked when they feel or do any of the following in the group:

- feel inadequate
- feel scared
- talk a lot
- feel uptight or anxious
- feel protective of someone
- feel threatened
- feel a need to correct a participant
- feel their face getting red
- feel they're doing more work than the group is
- feel defensive
- defend information
- feel angry
- repeat the same information a number of times

- spend an undue amount of time with one participant
- find themselves turning away from or ignoring a participant
- dread having to respond to a certain participant
- feel that the group is a drain rather than a joy

Games—the Vehicle for Getting Hooked

The vehicle for getting and staying hooked is a game. It takes two to play a game, so if you don't play, you won't stay hooked.

Participants also play games.

The following are games participants might play.

Yes, But

In this game, the following is communicated by a participant: *"I'd really like to do what you suggest, but I can't because my board of directors (or partner, or boss) won't let me."*

Rescuer

A participant says to another participant, *"I think you're doing everything right. You don't need to feel bad or do anything different."*

Tell Me to Do Something

A participant says to you, *"Look, just tell me what to do!"* or says to you, *"Don't you have any ideas about what I can do to deal with this problem with my employee?"*

Ain't It Awful?

The attitude in this game is expressed as follows: *"OMG, you have teenagers too?! How can you live with them? They don't do anything you ask them to do. Can't we just send them away to some island somewhere and bring them back when they're twenty-one?"*

I'm an Expert
A participant says to you or another participant, *"Look, I have a degree in human resource development and have worked in the field for ten years, so I know that what you're suggesting won't work. The most recent research tells us that employees aren't allowed to do that."*

Stupid
A game player of this type might say, *"Gosh, I'd like to do that. I don't have a degree and am just an administrative assistant. You might be expecting too much of me. I'm not aggressive like that."*

Now I've Got You
A game player of this type might say something to you like, *"In the first session, you told us to listen to our staff; now you're telling us to ignore them. Which is it? You are so confusing."* Or you might hear, *"You talk about listening, but I don't feel that you listen to me at all."*

You Are Wonderful!
You may hear something like this from someone who plays this sort of game: *"How do you know all of this? You're much younger than I am. I knew you were special, but I didn't realize how special. I could read tons of books and never understand things like you do!"*

Broken Leg
Someone who plays this sort of game may say something like, *"I wish I could do more at work. I don't think I told you, but my boss undermines everything I do."* or *"I can't do that because I might get fired."*

Why Do People Play Games?

We briefly introduced the idea that people play games because they don't want to take action or make a change. Many of us would do anything possible to maintain the status quo. Change is inevitable and although it is part of life, it can be hard.

With most of our groups, participants are attending voluntarily because they want to learn new behaviors. You would think that would be enough for people not to play games, but it isn't. The problem is that change is a journey into the unknown, and that can be scary, particularly when it is a self-journey. Leaving our comfort zones is vital, though, if we are to grow and change.

Change is tough for all of us. Even when people have signed up for a class and paid for it, they still can play games. They may consciously want to change their behavior for the better, but unconsciously they might play games. Think of the excuses you tell yourself or others when you don't want to stick to your diet, or go to the gym, or visit your partner's relatives. It's part of being human.

Remember, though, you as a facilitating leader are an agent of change. It's your job to help participants in your groups gently move toward change to better their lives. That's why they are there.

How to Avoid Getting Hooked

How can you avoid getting hooked? Or if you are hooked, how can you deal with it in the most constructive manner? Your first step is to recognize your own hooks. They vary from individual to individual. Following are some suggestions for how not to get hooked:

- o Actively listen to the other person's feelings.
- o Ask clarifying questions.
- o Agree—"You're right."
- o Don't respond at all. Nod perhaps to let the person know you've heard him or her.
- o Send an I-message—the word *I* plus what you are feeling or what you need.
- o Continue listening and say, "Uh-huh."
- o Call it a game. "I sense that you don't feel that anything will work."

    o   Do not defend yourself or your material.

    o   Use phrases like these—

-    "What would you like to do?"
-    "Can you tell me more about that?"
-    "It seems that you have a lot of feelings."
-    "You disagree with what I said." (Said as a statement.)
-    "I see it differently."
-    "That's interesting."
-    "That's not been my experience."
-    "I think your question will be answered next week when we talk about ____."

Don't be upset or show any discomfort nonverbally. When we are anxious, our posture often is closed up. The opposite is true when we're excited—we're opened up. So when you feel anxious, open up. You might fool your body into expressing a more neutral or positive feeling.

You're Human, and You Might Get Hooked Sometimes, so if You Do …

- Accept it. Give yourself permission to make mistakes.
- Talk it over with other people.
- Look for options for not getting hooked next time.
- Treat yourself to something special—ice cream, a warm slow bath, a walk in the woods, a talk with a friend or partner.
- If you're co-leading and a particular person seems to hook you a lot, have your co-leader answer all his questions and deal with him every session.

CHAPTER 15

THE BIG PICTURE

Building the Group and Keeping the Group

In this chapter, we delineate several best practices for effective group leading. Some of them we have described before; we will reinforce them in this chapter.

At the end of the chapter, we describe the big picture for change-making group facilitation. Here we present three overarching goals for effective group leaders – the three P's. These three goals are:

1. As leaders, we create a safe place to *protect* participants so they can freely pursue their own journey of self-discovery.
2. We establish a safe setting for the group by sending the message to group members that they have *permission* to say anything in the group while they are integrating skills.
3. We give participants the confidence to use the knowledge and skills you present in group. This type of confidence can be called *potency*.

The following are additional best practices for group leadership.

Build the Group

Decide before your group starts how you are going to implement an exercise or activity and "configure" group participants—in small groups, in pairs, half of the class, or the whole group.

If a participant can do something by herself, it is less threatening than doing it with one other person, which is less threatening than doing it with two other people, which is less threatening than doing it with four other people, which is less threatening than doing it with the whole group.

As a group facilitator, you have the responsibility to build the group so that each person participates in *every session* and feels fairly comfortable doing so. Create the "jumping in" to get group members' commitment. The longer a person waits to talk in group, the harder it is to get that person to invest in the group (and to get the group to invest in that person).

Break Up Subgroups

Break up subgroups (relatives who have come to group together; kids from the same class; good friends; coworkers from the same department; participants who constantly talk to each other during the sessions) within the group. Have them count off or choose the person they know least in the room, or have each member turn to the person to their left or right, or have members find someone who has a birthday in the same month as they have theirs.

Ask Participants to Talk Every Session

Have people speak at least once every session, even if it is to one other person. This reinforces commitment to the subject matter and the group.

Set Goals and Have an Agenda

State the goals for each session to the group, state what is going to be covered in that session, and prepare for the worst-and best-case scenarios for your group.

Accept and Decide

Group leading is an ongoing series of decisions that often must be made on the spot. Accepting group members does not mean that you agree with what is stated.

Keep in Mind the I, the We, and the It

Each session, keep the I, the We, and the It in mind, and try to keep these three elements somewhat balanced. The **I** is the individual participant and you as the leader; the **We** are the participants in the group, the group as a whole, and their interrelatedness; and the **It** is the topic or subject matter you are presenting during the session.

In terms of time and attention, these three elements need to be balanced, though they rarely are perfectly balanced. Your job as the group leader is to be the guardian of these three—the individual, the interrelatedness of the group, and the subject matter. Keep in mind that each element—the **I**, the **We**, and the **It**—needs to get equal attention as much as is possible.

Ruth C. Cohn in her article "The Theme-Centered Interactional Method" describes it this way: "The group process results from shifting balance the way a bicycle pitches because of the rider's shifting his weight from pedal to pedal. If perfect balance were ever achieved, the process would come to an end. The group leader's job is to employ his weight always toward the 'unused pedal,' that is, from 'I' to 'We' from 'It' to 'I,' and from 'We' to 'It.'"[4]

Note Similarities and Differences

Notice and celebrate similarities and differences. People identify with people who think like they do or have similar experiences or beliefs. Since you want the whole group to gel, be sure to point out differences

---

[4] Ruth C. Cohn, "The Theme-Centered Interactional Method," *Journal of Group Psychoanalysis and Process 2, no.2 (Winter 1969-1970)*

too. For example, "Susie and Tom's bosses said the same thing to them, but each of them responded differently to the experience."

Know Your Globe

To know your globe simply means that you know the physical environment where your group is meeting. Is it too small? Are there no chairs? Is there no Wi-Fi? Is it next door to the aerobics class with the loud music? Is it in the boiler room? Can you have food, coffee, and/or water in the room? Is there no heat or air-conditioning? Make sure you figure all these things out before meeting with your group.

Provide Examples and Responses

Forget the example you were going to use to clarify a point if a participant shares an example that makes the point you were planning to make.

Debrief

Debrief and discuss the highs, the lows and suggestions after each session, even if it's just with yourself.

Know Your Two Roles

As a group leader, be comfortable with the two roles that are key to using this approach: be a *leader* and a *facilitator*.

The Big Picture in Review—Protection, Permission, and Potency

The Importance of the 3 P's
There are three overarching goals we provide for the people in our groups, and every activity, exercise, didactic presentation, question, and response needs to address at least one of these three elements. They are the three P's—protection, permission, and potency.

How do we address the goals of protection, permission and potency in a group setting?

Keep the following in mind as you plan, lead and facilitate your groups.

Protection
Group leaders establish safety or *protection* for all participants and use "protection" strategies in several ways when their group meets. Here are some strategies for protecting group participants.

- Have faith in the goodness of your participants, and have faith that they have the best answers for their lives. Understand that feelings are an important ingredient in learning.

- Make sure participants know that they can pass if they don't want to answer a question or participate in an exercise.

- The fewer people to whom a person speaks, the less threatening it is to talk. Think of what it would be like to chat with your neighbor over the fence vs. addressing a group of 250 people. In your groups, ask participants to talk with one or two other people, particularly during Openers, to encourage each person's participation in the least threatening way.

- Protect participants by establishing rules and norms for what will happen and what to expect in the group and answering questions that might not be stated by participants, making sure you include the Transition phase of the Group Process Formula in every session.

- Group leaders keep in mind that they need to balance the I, the We, and the It to make sure no one is monopolizing the time or playing continuous games, playing the role of star participant or know-it-all.

- Implement Foreshadowing throughout the session to make bridges so participants know where they've been and where they are going.

- As a group leader, don't pass judgment.

- Share information about comfort and care, such as indicating where the bathrooms are and letting participants know if it is okay if they ask questions.

- Plan ahead and "know your globe."

- As a group leader, share the agenda with participants every session.

- Co-leading also contributes to protecting participants since there are two people planning together and, when the group meets, paying attention to what is going on with each participant in the group.

Permission

In our groups, we want all members to know that they can say anything they want and share their experiences, feelings, and values without being judged. Here are some strategies to promote group members' feeling that they have *permission* to share confidently in group.

- As a group leader, share your own experiences and personal examples and stories—both successes and nonsuccesses.

- Pay attention to nonverbal behaviors. Invite participants to share their experience, or try something else if you see that their nonverbal behavior indicates that they would like to do so.

- As a group leader, notice and celebrate similarities and differences, thereby lending both weight and respect to them.

- Throw out an open-ended question to the group rather than answering a question with the "right" answer.

- Using this model, participate in the exercises and activities you ask participants to engage in.

- Don't call on people; rather, ask them to volunteer.

- Highlight options and choices for participants.

- If there are personal disturbances, address them before moving on.

- Prioritize people first and the subject second.

- Encourage participants' talking to each other rather than through the leader.

Potency

We want participants to change their lives for the better according to their own journey of self-discovery. They need to feel confident or potent in order to change and try out new skills. Here are strategies to use in groups to increase the feeling of *potency* in members of the group.

- As a group leader, actively listen to participants.

- Assume an attitude of respect for all participants and their ideas, perspectives, values, and experiences. See them as part of the learning process.

- As a leader, "hold the hands" of participants in the first sessions to encourage confidence and competence.

- With the Group Process Formula, provide time and space for participants to practice skills before using them in their real-world situations.

- Call participants by name, and learn their names by the end of the first session.

- Refer to participants' examples and experiences, and bring them to the attention of the whole group.

- Push gently.

- As a group leader, have confidence in yourself and make sure you know your subject matter.

- Spend most of your time planning ahead of the group meeting.

- Develop exercises and activities that help participants feel good about themselves, other participants, and their competence.

- Believe that participants truly have the right answers for their lives.

As effective as we know the skills described within are, as well as the Group Process Formula, we realize that for most of us, they are not easy to implement. I often think of this book as a companion manual to our workshops.

For more information, please contact us at Haley Training Institute at joan@haleytraininginstitute.com or 412-508-6248 for more information about individual coaching, group workshops, train-the-trainer programs, or leadership training.

Thank you for your interest in Leadership through Group Process and Facilitating Skills *and happy, productive facilitating.*

Joan Haley

Printed in the United States
By Bookmasters